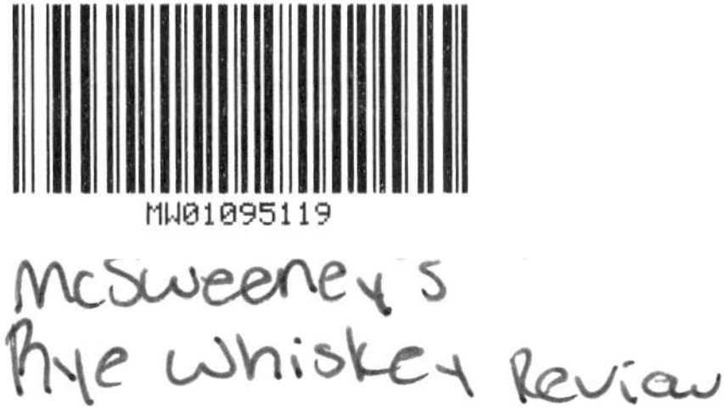

Composing Poetry:
A Guide to Writing Poems and Thinking Lyrically

Gerry LaFemina

Frostburg State University

Kendall Hunt
publishing company

www.kendallhunt.com
Send all inquiries to:
4050 Westmark Drive
Dubuque, IA 52004-1840

ISBN 978-1-4652-9581-1

Published in the United States of America

Table of Contents

Introduction: For Faculty v

1. About This Book 1
2. On Writing Poetry 5
3. How We Engage the Poem 15
4. A Crafted Thing 23

The Primary Modes of Poetry

5. On the Lyric Poem 31
   A. On the Personal Lyric Poem 34
   B. On the Observational Lyric Poem 49
6. On the Narrative Poem 65
7. On the Meditative Poem 89
8. On the Dramatic Poem 117
9. On the Post-lyric/Fractal Poem 137

Afterthoughts

10. No Ideas but in Things 161
11. Elegies 177
12. Performance Poems 191
13. Final Thoughts 215

Appendices

1. The Five Tool Poet 219
2. On Meter 227
3. Rookeries and Red Wheelbarrows 229
4. A (Very) Brief Discussion of Traditional Form 237
5. Additional Reading 241

Works Cited 243
Index of Poets and Titles 245
Permissions 249

Chapter One: About This Book

This book. This book in your hand. This book you're reading. This is a book about poetry. Not about sonnets and haiku—though surely about sonnets and haiku. Not about iambs and spondees. There are a number of fine books that will teach you the mechanics of form and meter.

No, this book is about poetry with regards to how poems think. And how they ask us to think when we read them. And how, as writers of poems, we want to help our readers think. See, I don't believe people who *think differently* write poetry, but rather writing and reading poems helps teach us to think differently.

Unlike other books on writing poetry, this book attempts to discuss a few of the basic strategies a poet might employ to bring a poem to life. We'll also talk about some of the essential skills—the importance of the image, for instance, and the development of the poet's ear—because a poem is about both the skills of the poet and the strategy the poet employs. It's an engineered device made of words, that, when done right, makes us feel something.

This is not a book on forms; there are plenty of guides in print and online for writing sonnets and villanelles. Nor is this a book of writing prompts and exercises. Again, there are plenty of books and web sites to help get you writing; to help you with shape and content. Poems are about both subject *and* form, but they're also about the poem's endeavor—what the poem does with subject and form. Therefore, this book is designed to help you consider what you *want* a poem to do with the content you have; how to shape it so the poem effectively reflects how you want your reader to experience it. Furthermore, knowing what you want a poem to do will help shape your voice as a poet.

For instance, there are lots of ways to write about love. One way is to try to make the reader understand how we feel, to try to use a metaphor to help re-create our experience of being "in love." One might be *to tell the story* of the first date we had with our beloved. Another might be ~~is~~ to think about all the ways we've experienced love, how it's never been the same experience, and thus attempt to understand the amorphous nature of love itself. Another might be to tell the story of love from someone else's point of view with the hope that it gives us insight into our own relationship.

What we've just discussed in the brief paragraph above are the lyric, narrative, meditative and dramatic possibilities of handling subject matter. That's what this book is about: how these four key ways of thinking can help shape and create the poems we write, how these types of poems differ from each other, and how they shape and create the experience our readers have when reading our poems.

Of course, nothing is that simple, but having a fundamental understanding of some of these basic concepts provides us with a foundation on which to develop our poetic voices and our poetic visions.

With all this in mind, the goal of this book is to teach some essentials of prosody (the craft of poetry writing) simultaneously with the rhetorical strategies poets employ. To do that we will examine how writing of poems is a means of thinking, and how to read poems like a writer because reading poems teaches us about writing poems. Just as guitarists listen to songs differently than non-musicians, so poets read poetry differently.

Reading as a Writer

Reading a poem as a writer is different than reading as a critic or scholar. Critics look at texts and their relationships to critical paradigms. Writers, on the other hand, look at finished poems as the result of choices—both conscious and unconscious—made by a poet. Poets read poetry with an eye to craftsmanship in order to learn more about the potentialities of craft in making meaning.

When we talk about poetry, often the first thing most people want to talk about is its content. People want to discuss the subject matter, what they see as "story" and, therefore, on the emotion of what's in the poem. But that's like saying that a house is only about who lives there. Like a house, a poem is a structure, it is architectural, it exists on a vertical and horizontal plane (the number of lines and the length of each line). A house dictates how we live in it—its rooms, its floor plan, etc., all force us to place our furniture in it in particular ways. Ditto, a poem's structure helps us figure out how to shape content. Poets see form the way architects see structure.

In order to do this, writers have to read "closely," which means writers read with attention paid to the construction of the poem, not just the content. Why? If a poem were just about its subject matter, why not then write it as a paragraph? Why write it as a poem? This is the first of a writer's many choices. From there, the poem is a series of choices that help give content more meaning, more power, more energy.

There's an old expression among poets, "Form enacts meaning," which means that form may help us understand a poem. By reading closely, writers read to see how the elements of craft help shape meaning

But form is not the only aspect of craft poets read for. They look for the "hot spots" of sound, word choice, imagery, diction, tone, etc. Poems are written to provide us a variety of ways to emphasize the meaning of the poem.

You're going to work on cultivating the skill of close reading in order to write better poems. Find poems you like and ask what it is about the poems (aside from content) that you find particularly compelling, maybe a simile or an image or a word choice. One way to do this is to retype your favorite poems: hitting enter at each line break will force you to see each end-word and to feel the length of each line. Doing this asks you to attend to each word, and thus to hear the sounds of each syllable more clearly. Another way of doing this is to read poems aloud.

As you read the poems included in these pages, consider not just the *what* of each poem but the *how* of them. Once you can decipher the ways in which the words on the page are a poem, you can learn from it. You can challenge yourself to use these technique in ways that suit your own needs and the needs of your poems.

Chapter Two: On Writing Poetry

Like many people I know, like many of the students I've taught, I began writing poems to express how I felt. The notion that poetry is a form of self-expression is as old as poetry itself: Sappho, the great Greek love poet, wrote her feelings for the women she loved. "The Song of Songs" is the expression of one man's passion for his beloved. Catullus wrote his contempt and desire. These poets and so many others like them felt something, and they needed to express that feeling. That said, though, a poem isn't solely self expression; such writing is called a diary entry or a journal page. No, a poem is expression mediated by the formal aspects of poetry and the self-conscious notion that we are writing a poem. A poem, after all, is a crafted thing. It has form and structure. It is an act of the imagination, which means to put experience into *image*, to make metaphor, to make symbol.

The poet Gregory Orr in *Poetry as Survival* states that poetry gives each of us a means to control the chaos that comes into our lives. We feel overwhelmed, and through the controlling aspects of language and form and expression, we are able to lasso in our feelings. Through poetic expression, we control the emotions that are causing the chaos within us. The poem, therefore, is not telling the reader *how* we feel, but rather tries to recreate through the poem the feeling itself.

What we try to do then, when we write a poem, is not communicate what we feel, but rather share *how* we feel. We do this using the precision of language, the power of the image, the musicality of phrasing, and the manipulation of the various tools poetry affords. These skills take years to master, and we master them in two ways. First , we must see these various aspects of craft enjoyed and employed well by other poets. Just as a young basketball player might watch NBA games and see how Lebron James handles the ball, just as a young artist walks through museums to study paintings, just as a young guitarist listens to guitar-heavy songs, so must a novice poet read poems. We learn (and we learn language in particular) both consciously and unconsciously. Reading poems helps us learn the "grammar" of individual poems, and we absorb such lessons so that we might try to employ them in our own poems.

The second way we achieve mastery of poetic skills is by attempting to write in ways that employ various poetic devices, forms, and modes. By doing so we start to identify not only our strengths and weaknesses as a young artist, but we tend to become comfortable with ourselves as poets. We begin to develop our individual voice as a poet. Our poetic voice is the aspect of ourselves in the poems we write, it is *who we are* in the poem. Just as we might speak a different way among our friends than we do with our grandparents, just as we might use different language and diction when we are in the workplace than on the basketball court, so, too, we "speak" differently in our poems than we do in our emails or in a composition essay. By mastering various poetic skills, we develop our poetic voice.

Voice is a combination of personal lexicon, our ability to use our poetic toolbox, and our ambition for the poems we write, which includes the *type* or *mode* of poetic inquiry we're engaging in; we might think of this as part of our artistic vision, and it is often a reflection of who we are and of how we think. One of the goals of this book is to help us experiment with a variety of poetic modes, such as the lyric, narrative, and meditative, in order to further our development of an individual poetic voice and vision.

Many years ago, PBS ran a series of television shows about American poetry called *Voices & Visions*. Each episode focused on one great American poet, and I think that name, *Voices & Visions*, sums up nicely what poetry becomes about for each of us who write it. Voice and vision share a symbiotic relationship within the work of each writer. Vision shapes the types of poems you write. Your voice, as embodied in the poems, hones and develops your vision.

As you write, you think through your subject matter, embody that thinking in language, and shape it with lines. Graham Wallas in *The Art of Thought* mentions a little girl who "had the making of a poet in her" because on "being told to be sure of her meaning before she spoke, [she] said, 'How can I know what I think till I see what I say'" (106). Wallas seems to agree that poets think as they say. By giving your thoughts voice, your vision is refined and defined *as your own*. Poetry is an art where your solitary voice and your solitary vision fuse in the making of each poem.

Early on in your writing, though, you often don't have a clear or distinctly individual voice. Your vision isn't clear yet, either. Beginning writers often think "big picture," rather than in the details of the world. They are told to write what they know, but not how to leap beyond the self into the imagination. What you know only takes you to the edge of mystery. The next step is to envision what you don't know based on the empiricism of what you've seen, what you've heard, what is possible. Novice writers are taught various forms but not how to use the poem to help them find their vision, how to use it to shape their voice. It takes time, truly, to discover the intricacies of poetry, to learn the various ways it might be used, and the various ways it helps formulate what it is you mean to say. That's rocky terrain. It means you have to acknowledge that you don't know what you want to say just yet. You have to begin in uncertainty, in a world that often seems filled with talking heads who appear so certain as to what's right and wrong. That's why it's good to remember that poets tend to learn more from poetic failures than successes.

You must also remember to trust the poetic process and your ability to actually find something to say. Writing in this way allows voice and vision to be interwoven. In one of the first books of literary criticism, *The Literary Mind & The Carving of Dragons*, the Chinese scholar Liu Hsieh notes that poetry is a combination of fruits and flowers. By fruit he means that what is said that is sustaining, in other words, content. Flowers refers to how content is said. A good poem has lots of fruit and lots of flowers, vision *and* voice.

There is an old saying: "I need to compose my thoughts." This is often used as a way of saying I must order them so that I can articulate them well. But what if there's a way to actually make new thoughts? Recent brain science tell us that we can "rewire" the neural pathways so that you can think along different routes. Composing a poem is one way to rewire your thinking process, so that when writing a poem, you are thinking differently (literally!) than when you're writing a text message, when you're in conversation, or when you're drafting a history paper.

More importantly, the writing of each poem might require different thinking. Consider how a 26-line abercedarian (an acrostic poem in which each line starts with the next letter of the alphabet) must be essentially different from a haiku, not just in its length and breadth, but in the strategy of its thought process because of those differences. The strategies and styles of poems you feel comfortable writing says much about who you are as a poet and what you want a poem to do.

Poetry, then, provides ways to think, using the tools of craft so that you may better articulate and even formulate a personal vision. You develop your poetics, as it were: what poems mean to you, by learning what is possible using language and line, metaphor and meter, and numerous other tools. Even the tools you choose to employ regularly, say something about your voice and vision; so, too, do the tools you use infrequently.

So what are some of these skills? This becomes tricky territory. Different poets would say different things. Over the course of your poetry career, you might find that the line is important at one point and image at another. Just as a young baseball player might find that fielding is an important skill in little league, hitting is an important skill in high school, and base running an important skill later in the minors, a poet will discover that certain skills become important at different stages of her career. Furthermore, just as a baseball player may have certain strengths and weakness, ditto a poet may have some natural strengths that need to be honed, and weaker skills that need to be developed.

For this reason, it's important to discuss five broad features a poem needs to be successful. Done well, the poem might have what the Spanish poet Federico Garcia Lorca, called *duende*: a "mysterious power that all may feel and no philosophy can explain." All art should have this soul. Our task is to consider how an author used the elements of poetry to create a text with duende, and, more importantly, how might we do something similar in our own work. In baseball, the five-tool player can hit for average, hit for power, run the bases well, field well, and throw. In poetry, five tools are similarly important. **For a fuller discussion on the five tools of poetry, see appendix 1.**

The first tool is the centrality of lyricism and the lyric experience. By lyric, we mean a personal stance that conveys the ecstatic—that experience of momentarily being taken out of ourselves (emotionally, spiritually, sexually, psychologically, artistically, etc.). There are five main rhetorical modes we can employ to express such experiences:

a. **Lyric** Lyric poems capture the lyric event, often a small moment, without much (or any) story at all. The poem engages only the sensibility of the "event." As Kenneth Koch says "the point may only be to get into that poem the look of a locust tree in the early spring" (9).

b. **Narrative** Narrative poems relate stories, often the story of the lyric event.

c. **Meditative** Meditative poems reflect upon the significance of an object or event while making connections to narrative, outside knowledge, other experiences, and the illustrations of abstract thought.

d. **Dramatic** In the dramatic or persona poem, the author employs the personal stance of a character, fictive or realistic, and the poem concerns itself with that character's sensibilities.

e. **Fractal** The fractal poem (or post lyric poem) formally enacts the fractured nature of lyric experience rather than trying to order it, allowing the poem to have multiple voices, temporalities, and viewpoints.

This book explores these modes of handling the lyric experience, and each highlights different strengths of an individual poet.

The second tool is an awareness of the image and its central importance to a poem. When we write using our imagination, essentially we are putting thought into images. A cornerstone of poetry, image is fashioned from words that convey concrete, sensory experiences for the reader. William Carlos Williams said "No ideas but in things." By this he meant that an abstraction (love, for instance) exists not in the word but in how it's manifested in the world—in action, in item, in *thing.*

Image goes beyond mere description. It communicates a feeling or phenomena so vividly that it enters a reader's mind and allows them to experience the sensations. While the word "image" suggests most obviously a visual or picture, it includes any sensory experience of smell, sound, touch, and taste. Figurative language (simile, metaphor) associates unlikely things to create a concrete description for the otherwise inexpressible experience or sensation. For this reason, Aristotle said that metaphor is the most important skill for a poet. Furthermore, the images we use and how we present them can help develop the poem's tone.

All readers come to any poem with "schema," that memory-knowledge that helps us understand the world and any text we encounter. Therefore, in addition to its more tangible initial impact, effective imagery has the potential to tap the reader's inner wisdom, to arouse meditative and inspirational responses. Tension in a poem can be created by using contrasting images or contrasting sensory experience.

The third tool of poetry involves our use of, and ability to give attention to language. Samuel Coleridge said that poetry is the best words in the best order, but that leads us to questions: what makes a word the best? And how do we string them together in a way that is better than another way? As we work a poem through the compositional process, we look to answer those questions.

Sometimes we might think that the bigger the word, the more complicated our diction, the more convoluted the sentences, the better the poem, the *deeper* and more intelligent the speaker appears. However, such words often call attention to themselves and may force the reader out of the moment presented

> One of the most important skills for any artist, whether one is making a poem or baking a cake (a high art form indeed!), is an attention to details. Artists pay attention to the details. Too much baking powder in the cake batter and your oven is a mess. Too much salt and not enough sugar might make your cake inedible. Leave your cake in the oven for too long and the fire department might show up. Most of all, it's important to consider your audience: you wouldn't bake a chocolate cake for your son's birthday if he were allergic to cocoa. Ditto, recognizing who your readers are is important when composing and editing your poems.

in the poem to wonder why the poet used such an alien, awkward-sounding, or archaic word. There's a thin line between artistry and artifice, and (in general) a poem strives for seamless artistry. As your voice and your vocabulary are critically linked, using language that feels organic to the speaker's voice is important in making a successful poem. The power of the poem, in many ways, has to do with the intimate interaction between the poem's speaker and the audience, between poet and reader.

Remember, Japanese haiku masters created hauntingly beautiful poems with only 17 syllables and often the simplest language in part because poems are as much about how we use words as it is the words we use.

Much has been made about poetry's relationship to song: the notion of the lyric poem and the song lyric being the most obvious connection. **The fourth tool** at the poet's disposal is attention to the sonic interaction or sounds of the spoken poem. Always remember that the roots of poetry are in the oral tradition (for the poet), and it remains an aural art form for the audience; we all have that voice in our head who reads to us. The nature of the sonic resources used by poets convey and can reinforce the meaning or experience of poetry. Sonic effects often appear in combination, and devices that contribute to the creation of sound include alliteration, assonance, consonance, rhyme (including internal rhyme, half-rhyme), onomatopoeia, cacophony, rhythm, and meter.

To better understand the effects of sonic interaction in a poem, consider Gerard Manley Hopkins's "Pied Beauty" by reading it aloud. Listen for the complicated sounds of the poems, and feel how your mouth moves to say these lines. You will hear alliter-ation, end rhyme, internal rhyme, cacophony, meter, and more:

Glory be to God for dappled things—
    For skies of couple-color as a brinded cow
        For rose-moles all in stipple upon trout that swim
    Fresh-firecoal chestnut-falls; finches' wings
        Landscape plotted and pierced—fold, fallow and plow;
            And all trades, their gear and tackle and trim.
    All things counter, original, spare, strange;
        Whatever is fickle, freckled (who knows how?)

With swift, slow; sweet, sour; adazzle, dim;
He fathers-forth whose beauty is past change:
Praise him.

The language's richness in sound, particularly in some of the original pairings of words and the proximity of sonic combinations, makes the poem stand out.

The last tool of the poet's trade is an attention to form and structure. Because verse defies the traditional prosaic phrasing of a paragraph, the poem's architecture becomes especially important how we experience it. First and foremost, poems are written in lines, and attention to the line affords a variety of strategies for the poet to manipulate meaning, sound play and more. **For more on the line, see appendix 3.**

Lines are a poem's girders: they are the structural support of both the poem and the voice of the speaker. The fact that poems appear in lines distinguishes poetry from prose, and therefore, considerations for where we end the line (where the line *breaks*) is the first of many formal concerns we might make about a given poem. Early on, the line was often decided by a poem's formal requirements (a sonnet asks for a five beat line in iambic feet, aka iambic pentameter); however, since the birth of free verse, what makes a line is determined by the poet and the poem.

Robert Frost once said that writing free verse is akin to playing tennis without a net. Many formalist poets like to suggest that this is a criticism of free verse, i.e., it's easy to play tennis without a net. On the other hand, one might consider that if we choose to play tennis without a net, then we have to make up rules for how we're going to play, and they may be based on how big of a court area we have, the equipment we have, time constrictions, the light, and numerous other concerns. Are we going to have to return the ball on the fly? On one hop? On two? In other words, if we're going to write free verse, then we're going to have to think about the lines we're writing. It may be *free* after all, but it's still *verse.*

Now that we've discussed the basic poetic tools, some things need to be clarified. These are skills that are developed and honed.

A person may have a natural gift with metaphor, so his early strength may include image making, while another novice writer may be gifted with an interest in language play and therefore her early strength may be in the sonic attention she gives a poem. Somebody else may be great at telling stories, while another person might be able to capture small, powerful moments. These skills are starting points, and comparing our skill sets to that of others can often be disheartening. It takes time to develop into a five-tool poet. As Aristotle said, we train ourselves to be excellent. Working on poems, drafting a poem over and over again to find those best words and their best order, is one way we become closer to excellence.

No one expects a poet to write with all five tools employed at the same time. The "writing" of a poem happens in drafts, it's honed and touched up. Some people write a poem in prose blocks and then look to find its line; other people may choose to add figurative flourishes in later drafts. It can be very frustrating to look at a well-established poet's work because we're seeing a final draft, one that may not only have been worked over multiple times by the poet herself, but also may have been sent to a friend for input, then had an editor make some suggestions. Just as the final version of a movie has scenes left on the cutting room floor, or the final version of a song has multiple "takes" that we've never heard, so too is a poem written in drafts, and each draft permits us to bring a different set of tools to the page.

Chapter Three: How We Engage the Poem

Early on in "Song of Myself" Walt Whitman declares "what I assume you shall assume,/For every atom belonging to me as good belongs to you." What he is really saying is that he wants you to share the experience of the poem with him, that in reading the poem, you, too, "loafe in the grass." That's a big declaration, but it's also what every poet tries to do: to not tell of an experience, but to create one, to share one with the reader, so that upon reading we might feel as Emily Dickinson said about poems: "If I read a book and it makes my whole body so cold no fire can warm me, I know that is poetry. If I feel physically as if the top of my head were taken off, I know that is poetry. These are the only way I know it. Is there any other way?"

Poetry, in other words, isn't always about "getting it," it's about feeling it. Poets use language to shape how we feel and how we think when we read their poems. There's a reason poetry writing is considered *creative* writing. Poetry is not so much a way of reporting what has happened as it is a way of creating an event for the reader. We do this in many ways—by word choice, by the images used, by the look of the poem, by its form and meter, surely. But it's also created by the poem's strategy, by the mode of thinking the poem employs, and the rhetorical strategies each mode demands.

By rhetoric, I mean nothing more than how the Greeks thought of it, "the art of using language for persuasion, in speaking or writing; especially in oratory" (747). Persuasion, though, is such an ugly word. Perhaps it's better to say "the art of using language to get our audience to participate in something beyond themselves." Poems use three primary rhetorical sensibilities—what I call modes—to help the audience have an experience, and these modes have existed since the dawn of poetry. They are the lyric, the narrative, and the meditation. The dramatic mode (that poem written in the voice of somebody else) draws upon these other three, and some newer, postmodern sensibilities, such as the fractal, are reactions to the primacy of lyricism. The most important thing to know at this juncture is that the way subject matter in the lyric, narrative, and meditative poem is engaged is somewhat different.

The lyric tends to deal with the invocation of a moment, the narrative tends to tell a story, and the meditation tends to explore one's thinking on a particular subject.

Of course, nothing is so clean. And *lyricism* is a key component of all of these modes, just as water vapor is the key component of all clouds; poems can use elements of both the narrative and the lyric. Luke Howard, who set up the first classification of clouds, understood something similarly: sure there were cirrus clouds, and cumulus clouds, and nimbus clouds, but there were also clouds that shared aspects of two types, the cumulonimbus cloud, for instance. So, too, are there lyric-narrative poems, all of which we get to later on in this book.

For now, let's return to the notion that a poem is a way of shaping thoughts and that poets use a variety of craft tools to mold how we experience what we read. This is why it's important when composing a poem not only to think like a writer but also to think like a reader. Some reactions happen before we even acknow-ledge the words on the page. Consider how you react to a poem that is three-pages long as opposed to a haiku. A poem's length, the length of its lines, its shape on the page, whether its made up of one long stanza or multiple stanzas, its use of indentations—such decisions pace our eyes, control our mouth if

> Often people think poems are about subject matter; the fact is poems are about how we handle our subject matter—why else would we choose to write it as a poem? Different types of poems provide us with different strategies to engage our material. Sylvia Plath in "Daddy," Robert Hayden in "Those Winter Sundays," and Sharon Olds in her book *The Father* (among so many others!) each engage a dysfunctional relationship between a child and a father. The details brought to the poems, the imagery and language, the poetic strategies employed, and the way each writer handles craft, makes each poem unique, memorable, and powerful. Remember: poems are about how we say it as much as they are about what we say.

we're reading the poem aloud (and it's always good to read a poem aloud), and determine what we are in for as readers.

Give the poem below a quick glance without reading the words. Consider what your expectations are when we see a poem that looks like this:

The moon glimmering on green water.
White herons fly through the moonlight.

A young man hears a girl picking water-chestnuts:
into the night, singing, they paddle home together.

Those four long-ish lines in two couplets, do they shape your expectations at all? Do they serve a purpose? What did you think was coming? What does a poem so brief require of us when we begin? How does the brevity of what appears before us set up our expectation?

This poem is titled "Autumn River Song" by the Chinese poet Li Po. What assumptions does the title set up for us? How does the poem meet those expectations? How does it subvert them? Do you read it differently knowing that title? At only four lines, the poem has to do a lot of work in a short space.

These two couplets by Li Po ask us to give them only a brief amount of time—the twenty seconds or so required to read them. As such, the poem needs to astonish us, needs to engage us at the sensory level and cause a reaction, the way a bee sting makes us respond. *It makes my body so cold...*

Now think of what Whitman's "Song of Myself" asks of us when we just contemplate its 52 sections. This is not a walk around the block but rather a walk through the city, and just as we'd engage the latter walk differently, so, too, we engage Whitman's poem differently.

1

I celebrate myself, and sing myself,
And what I assume you shall assume,
For every atom belonging to me as good belongs to you.

I loafe and invite my soul,
I lean and loafe at my ease observing a spear of summer

grass.

My tongue, every atom of my blood, form'd from this soil,
this air,
Born here of parents born here from parents the same, and
their parents the same,
I, now thirty-seven years old in perfect health begin,
Hoping to cease not till death.

Creeds and schools in abeyance,
Retiring back a while sufficed at what they are, but never
forgotten,
I harbor for good or bad, I permit to speak at every hazard,
Nature without check with original energy.

We are in for a vastly different landscape of language and of the world. We know, just by looking at these lines of varied length, some so long they have to scroll down onto a second line, that reading this poem is a radically distinctive event for us.

And we haven't even looked at a word yet! Now consider the rhetorical choices of such poems. In the first poem, Li Po, engages the image directly; he thrusts us into the immediacy of the scene. There is no I delivering this information to us although we have an implied I telling us what he's witnessed. On the other hand, Whitman engages us in voice, in a conversation, and lets us know we are going to "loafe" along with him at his ease. The lyric I, that person talking, that singular voice, engages us, and we're going to be here for awhile. Better sit back and pay attention.

Even a short poem, though, demands our attention. Emily Dickinson's poems, with their ungrammatical capitalizations and use of dashes, ask us to pay attention despite their often orderly stanzas in a 4/3 rhythmic pattern (what is known as common meter) and use of end rhyme. Surely her poems *look*, at first glance, traditional. But her poems were so outside-the-box that when they were first published, the poems were "normalized" so that the dashes and capitalizations were changed. Dickinson's poems ask us to ask them questions. That's why we have to pay attention to our reading.

Another poem that's simultaneously untraditional and

traditional is this one by the Modernist poet Laura Elizabeth Richards.

Eletelephony (1932)

Once there was an elephant,
Who tried to use the telephant—
No! No! I mean an elephone
Who tried to use the telephone—
(Dear me! I am not certain quite
That even now I've got it right.)
Howe'er it was, he got his trunk
Entangled in the telephunk;
The more he tried to get it free,
The louder buzzed the telephee—
(I fear I'd better drop the song
Of elephop and telephong!)

The poem's title is a nonsense word. As with Dickinson, we see the dashes; we also get parentheticals that bring in the voice of the speaker editorializing on herself) and the use of dashes. The poem, though is written in rhyme and meter. The way these two different sensibilities work in the poem give it a certain silliness: it feels like a children's poem (which it is), but its syntax and style is not kiddie. As poets, it's important to remember the joy of language, the kind of clay that words can become. "Eletelephony" might be playful, but the poem's story of an elephant using a telephone might just be a metaphor for the use of traditional and modern techniques. Worlds collide.

Here's one more (I know, I know, I'm throwing a lot of poems at you but one way we become a better writer is by reading), this one a contemporary poem by Kathleen McGookey, "Like Stars."

I am walking when a small patch of overcast sky clears. It is almost evening, and the sun shines on white birds against darker sky. Just then, the insects stop buzzing and their silence feels like presence. The birds reflect the light like stars. Huge bright flocks move their weight across the sky. Right now my friend is having a baby boy who is expected to die.

What we notice right away is that this poem doesn't have any line breaks—it's what's called a prose poem. As such, it requires we approach it differently, as if it were an ordinary paragraph, which allows for its extraordinary use of imagery and its shocking ending to have that much more surprise. The lack of line breaks camouflages the poetic nature of the piece. Having it delivered to us as a declared poem may put us on even more uncertain footing as we ask, *huh? I thought a poem was written in lines, so why is this a poem?* Again, the poem announces to us that we're going to have to read this differently than the previous three.

This is true because the thinking of each poem is unique. And they were written differently, with individualized intents from the get go. The writers had to pay attention to their delivery so that readers know how attentive they need to be as they enter the poem. Poet Paul Muldoon puts it succinctly when he says, "As a reader I am standing in for the 'writer' of the poem. I am shadowing him or her in the process of determining from word to word and from line to line the impact of those words and those lines" (218).

Sometimes, before a longer poem, I might want to clear my head for a moment, or shut off my cell phone so it doesn't ring while I'm in the middle of it, whereas, with a short poem, I might be willing to take that chance (it's only four lines long, after all!)

All art asks us to pay attention. It's the fundamental skill of any artist and any afficionado. Don't pay attention while eating, and you might miss the subtleties of a particular dish. Don't pay attention at the museum, and you might miss how the brush strokes move toward a space on the canvas the painter intends for us to focus on. Don't pay attention at the basketball game, and you might miss a terrific dunk. Don't pay attention to the poem, and you might miss the best word in the best order. This is equally true for the artist/writer. We are, after all, asking the reader to give the poem we are writing her attention, so don't we owe it to her to give the poem as much attention as we can? The more we invest in the poem, the more we can ask the reader to invest, and if we don't give it our attention, well you know what might go wrong. Don't pay attention while painting, and your dog looks more like a horse. Don't pay attention while writing and your reader may be bored or lost.

This is about intent.

All art work has intention. We often think that intention comes first, but often it doesn't. Often in the process of making art we understand our intentions. Art is a way of processing experience, of distilling it, of *thinking* about it. The poetic art is a way of thinking about it by shaping its language that is both simultaneously ordinary and extraordinary. The best poems sound like the self we dream ourselves to be—by giving us the opportunity to revise our language, to hone it, to sculpt it and shape it, to manipulate aspects of craft, we get to bring an experience into being for ourselves and for our readers.

The American philosopher John Dewey claimed that art was *the experience*. It was his view that people seeing art should have something akin to the experience that the artist had while making the art work. What we've crafted should also allow for the reader's imagination to follow along, to assume what we assumed when writing.

Chapter Four: A Crafted Thing

I tell my students a poem is a crafted thing. By this I mean poets consider elements of poetry in the making of poems, and as such the making of a poem is a process. One of the biggest myths that young poets believe is the notion that a sonnet is composed in rhyme (as opposed to is edited toward rhyme), that the poet uses a process to come up with the final fourteen lines. Why is this a bad myth to believe?

Let's say a poet writes these two lines for a sonnet they've just started writing:

Among the empty cans left from last night,
among the cigarettes and detritus....

Well, now we have a problem, the next line has to rhyme with *detritus*. A good poet may surprise us (*surprise us*: that would rhyme!) with what he or she comes up with, they would then have to rhyme something with *night*. So they consider all the words that they can think of *at that moment* that rhyme with night (might, right, light, spite, blight, flight, tight, incite...) and thus limit the scope of the poem's next line (and thus the direction the poem might take) to the rhyming words. The other way to approach the sonnet, is to write the poem without the formal requirements at the forefront of our thoughts and then shape it, sculpt it, to fit the form.

For instance, "detritus" established a mood. If I change *detritus* to *memories* the poem's mood is transformed, but also my possible rhyming words. It's a change I couldn't make if I wedded myself early on to rhyming *detritus* throughout the sonnet.

But, as I said before, this book isn't about writing sonnets, although talking about sonnets allowed me to talk about crafting, about the types of choices poets make, and when in the process poets make such choices. We've already talked about the tools of the writer, and we've already talked about how poems think. Now it's important to remember that the crafting of the poem, the honing of the poem, also shapes of how we think.

Writing sonnets can teach us a bit about prosody, but often, focusing on writing in a fixed form makes the writing about the form and not the content. The fact is that there is no template for writing a good poem: every lyric poem is different. The sonnet is a great form for a lyric poem. As is the villanelle. As is free verse. The form of the poem, in the end, is a container for what's said, and it provides the poet with different strategies to express that content: the constriction of rhyme and meter and line length in the sonnet, the constriction of rhyme and repetition in the villanelle, the constriction of our own rules in free verse.

Still, understanding the aspects of craft that the writing of villanelles and sonnets (and other fixed forms) provides teaches us a great deal about what we can do with free verse. Our jobs as writers is to create a poem that uses craft to make the poem resonate with the reader. As Keats noted, "Poetry should surprise by a fine excess .... It should strike the reader as a wording of his own highest thoughts, and appear almost as a remembrance." That's why people read poetry. That's why we revise and edit as writers.

We agree, after all, that poetry is an art. Artists need talent, but they also need to hone their natural abilities. Almost anyone playing guitar goes to lessons to learn scales and chords, fingering, and the rudimentaries of musical theory. Novice guitarists learn a lot of songs (some they may want to play and some they wish they could skip!), in order to develop a working knowledge of the skills. Even a self taught guitarist

> After paying attention, one of the most important skills a poet can have is dedication. Writing poems, as with any art, requires discipline, discipline to master and keep in shape the skills we have, and to work on the skills we still need. One of the hardest things for an artist is that early on in the study of the art, mastery of new skills comes quickly, and we are often able to see our growth as a writer: we'll write a poem we couldn't have written six weeks before; later, development happens more slowly, and it may take months, or even years, for us to write a poem that reflects such growth. Dedication and faith in the process are crucial to our becoming better poets.

(working with a chord book or YouTube) is learning different skills and honing her craft. She is also, no doubt, listening to music; it may be that hearing some guitar music made her want to be a guitarist. Without study and practice, a guitarist isn't going to master the craft of guitar playing.

Because poetry uses language, and because almost everyone uses language everyday, the assumption is anyone can write poetry. And everyone *can* write something that we may call poetry, just as anyone with a pencil and paper *can* draw something. No one would take my ill-formed stick figures and call them art, however.

We study poetic craft, then, to distinguish between the artistry of being a poet and being someone who writes in verse, just as we take drawing class to distinguish ourselves from someone who doodles (poorly). We do it by reading and by writing, and by reading as a writer. (If you ever listened to Jimi Hendrix with a serious guitar player, you understand she's listening to the songs in a different way than a non-guitarist is listening). Many times, we go to poetry class with some skills and having been told that we're good writers—good poets, even—, and then we learn everything we don't know and become frustrated. It's daunting. A student may come to class wanting more praise, though more often than not, the people who praised him don't read much poetry (if any!) and they're invested in the yong poet's feelings. Other students, though, want to face the challenge of what they don't know and hope to become better poets or else understand that the skills they learn studying poetry will help them in other writing. Like becoming a good guitarist, becoming a better poet requires practice and dedication, study and the willingness to fail. Make a meal that's so salty that nobody eats it, and you will never put so much salt in the dish again when you're making it next.

We study craft for another reason too. The German philosopher Georg Hegel praised poetry as one of the highest art forms because it used language, and therefore its goal was to communicate something (emotions, ideas, thoughts, experiences) to an audience. We write poems hoping someone will read them and that the poems will be meaningful. The question readers have for a poet becomes, in the end, why should we care about your subject matter? Why should *anybody* care about the subject matter of your poems? This isn't meant to be harsh, but rather it's just a reality check: you've asked the reader to spend time with your poem. If we are asking the reader to invest time and energy into reading the poem, we ought to have invested time and energy into the writing of it. Consider: how much time have you spent with your poem? And how have you rewarded the reader for giving his/her time to your work?

One of the things, therefore, that a poet must do is make sure the reader is engaged by the poem. It's not enough to just express yourself. The poet's job is to create an experience that the reader participates in. This doesn't happen by just expressing one's self. Instead, the goal of the poem is to invite the reader in so that (s)he feels a part of the event. The poem has to have tension and that tension needs to be relieved. This is why we have so many tools to use. We craft a poem because tension is found not only in subject matter but in how the poem is presented: its word usage, its line, its form, its sound, its imagery. A poem is a series of choices. It's a made thing. And the whole ought to be greater than the proverbial sum of its parts.

As mentioned previously, the great twentieth century Spanish poet Federico Garcia Lorca used the term *duende*. All art should have duende, something that makes it compelling and resonant. Unfortunately, there is no duende seasoning in the spice rack. There's no easy template for making a poem compelling. So how do we do it? Here are some possible ways:

- The poem is formally interesting: how the poem uses prosody (stanza, line, spacing on the page) is compelling due to heightened rhythmic and visual effect.
- The poem's subject is captivating, and the event brought to life by the poem has some level of imaginative/emotional/spiritual/psychological import that is conveyed urgently so that we're given insight into this existence.
- The poem provides insight into an experience that is new—there is little engaging about cliche, about the familiar and usual masquerading as a poem. Robert Frost (again): "No tears for the writer, no tears for the reader. Nothing new for the writer, nothing new for the reader." If you want us to read the poem, you have an obligation to give us something fresh (think of it in terms of dining out—the best meals are the ones

you wouldn't make at home).

- The poem holds a metaphor (or better yet, enacts a metaphor) that captures an experience in a surprising way; in other words, the poem makes a cognitive leap that bridges two things (the metaphor and a personal experience) in such a way as to make us feel something universal.
- The poem uses language in unique ways—a poem is composed of words and so it helps that our word choices (not *all of them*) show a care to be accurate to more than meaning alone.
- The poem shows, doesn't tell: the poem resists the urge to employ abstractions except when necessary—"nervousness compels him to pick at a scab" tells me less than "he picks a scab," which allows the reader to do some work.
- Lastly, the poem doesn't suffer from tunnel vision, but rather it has a counter weight to its thinking: a "but," something that challenges the reader and the poet to think beyond the poem's initial impulse.

As with any artistic medium, poets work in service to three masters: the self, the audience, and the art form, and the most important thing to realize is the self is the least important because the writer-self is inherently there: *you wrote the poem.* By the time the poem has been written and revised, the initial emotions and sensibilities that triggered the writing have been mediated. We are now allowing the poem to do the same for the reader—our audience is the second most important of the three. Without readers, our poems have no ambition, no rationale for craft, no reason to exist: they are diary entries. Therefore, we have an obligation to the reader to make them want to read the poem and to make the poem an experience. Most importantly, though, we serve the poem and, through it, the art of poetry. By using the techniques and elements of craft, we engage in an art form that goes back to the fire pits and cave days, that goes back to the shaman. We honor it and our humanness by treating the poem not as something written but rather treating it as an artifact.

The Primary Modes of Poetry

Chapter Five: On the Lyric Poem

Often when we talk about the lyric poem, people get confused as the term *lyric* can be defined as the words of a song as well as a type of poem. Both terms share a root: the Greek poems that were sung often with the accompaniment of a lyre, a small, stringed harp. Over the course of time, song lyrics and lyric poetry have come to mean different things. Song lyrics, for one, work in conjunction with instrumentation, melody, and rhythm—the words are one part of a bigger whole. Lyric poems rely solely on language to do the work of communicating mood and feeling. Over the last 150 years, poetry has distinguished itself from song lyrics by removing the emphasis of meter and rhyme—the trappings of "measures" in song—and focusing instead on the nexus of language's inherent musicality and the image's resonant possibility. Therefore, lyric poems often have a greater attention to each and every word than song lyrics. Another problem has to do with audience expectations: songs are often written to appease a public audience, whereas poems are often written as if engaging in an intimate conversation.

Poet David Kirby echoes many people on this subject when he defines the lyric poem as "a short personal poem" (97), but this feels inadequate in some ways. In *The Portrait of the Artist as a Young Man,* James Joyce suggested that the lyric is "the form wherein the artist presents his image in immediate relation to himself" (165). By this we mean that the lyric poem presents an aspect of the self filtered through the writing.

Earlier we said that lyric poems capture the lyric event, often a small moment, without much (or any) story at all. If we consider song lyrics again, many songs engage this notion of expressing a moment: when the Rolling Stones sing "Let's Spend the Night Together," they are talking about the feeling of the moment. True lyric poems capture these moments in ways that allow the reader to participate in the feeling. But it's more than just the expression of emotion, it's the *imaginative* rendering that makes a poem. As D.G. James put it: "What is poetical in a lyrical poem is not the mere presence of strong emotion and feeling, but the imaginative apprehension of them" (117), for it's the imaginative presentation that creates a shared space for the reader.

In general, a lyric poem is a short poem with a distinct voice, that tries to put a microscope to (to open up and reveal fully) a particular moment. (From now on, we'll call this sort of moment in a poem a **lyric moment**.) Poet Erica Dawson, when asked in one of my poetry classes as to why she opted to be a poet and not a novelist, put it this way: "What I realized is that I was interested in the moment, [and] not stringing those moments together." Narrative is the art of stringing those moments together, while lyric poetry is the art of the moment.

Metaphor, symbol, image, all help make the moment resonate, give us tangibles to help understand the intangible experience. Much of the importance of the image is rooted in the idea of the described object being endowed with lyric value in order to capture the moment of "seeing"this. The lyric moment in a poem resonates. Through the use of poetic language, it attempts to cre-ate an understanding within the reader—perhaps not intellectual, but visceral. Lyric poems may also capture an intellectual moment, a spiritual moment, a metaphysical moment, but always they are trying to generate some sense of understanding, in a brief way, within the reader. The philosopher-critic Eileen John suggests that many poems perform a kind of "thoughtwriting" so that a "a poem, in its particular verbal and structured form, spells out the content and flow of a line of thought, such that the reader can think what the poem says. The poem can be the script of the reader's thoughts" (460). The poem becomes, as it were, a metaphor for the experience itself.

The history of the lyric is filled with distinctive poems of the I; poet Gregory Orr suggests that every culture has a lyric poem because of the human need to express the unknown and overcome chaos. To be able to put it into language and thus "order" feelings that overwhelm us is an inherent need. Consider how many people write when they are sad or depressed; or why when they're ecstatic with love they write about it. There's a reason why there are so many love poems, so many elegies, so many cliches about writers who are crazy: writing allows us to express and to edit (or, better yet) clarify exactly what we feel. Although long over, the Romantic era's sensibility of the poetic I remains rooted, perhaps, in William

Wordsworth's notion that inspiration is found "in the spontaneous overflow of powerful feelings," which the poet works on when he can "recollect in tranquility." These days we might think that the lyric poem comes in two distinct forms: the personal lyric, where the I is in the foreground of the poem, and the observational lyric, in which the I is removed from the language of the poem, but whose voice and vision flavor how we are allowed to "witness" the lyric events.

The contemporary lyric comes out of this tradition, which is as old as Sappho's fragments, haiku, and the Song of Songs. The American poem—like America itself—comes from the great belief in the spirit of the individual and the engagement of community: Dickinson and Whitman. Add to it Imagism's belief in the power of remaking how we experience something, and John Dewey's view that art is an experience, we get a notion that a lyric poem ought to have a distinct music and strong imagery to allow the reader entrance into the experience being described.

Much of the lyric sensibility is found in "associative" thinking as opposed to "temporal" or narrative thinking. The image/metaphor becomes an associative symbol of the lyric experience. In his book *Leaping Poetry*, Robert Bly discusses the associative "leap" of the image and makes a claim that the power of poetry is often rooted in such gestures by making a (new) metaphor that associates a feeling or sensibility with something else, we ask the reader to follow along our thought process and figure out what is similar between these two dissimilar things. The lyric poem's power is in the breadth of those leaps.

By using other poetic strategies (such as narrative and meditation), the poet can engage the notion of lyricism for a variety of effects. What we see, as poetry evolves, is a poem in which the central tenets of the lyric can be "lit" within a longer poem (or a fragmented poem) in order to emphasize a poem's "themes" and possibilities.

Chapter Five A: On the Personal Lyric Poem

The personal lyric is one of the primary modes of poetry; every culture has a form of this lyric poem: the poem of the *I* which gives voice to the moment. Since the advent of Modernism (starting around 1900), the lyric poem has been the dominant mode of American poetry. The American lyric is characterized by the importance of a central image or set of images that help give concrete understanding to an abstract experience.

The goal of the personal lyric is to express emotion in ways that are fresh and force the readers to use their imagination (Don't forget: the root of the word "imagination" is "image") to participate in the poem's event. Lyric poems are intense, usually imagistic, and, more often than not, focused on a "moment": a moment in time, an emotional mo-ment, a spiritual moment. By mediating this feeling through the art of writing and editing, we allow ourselves some control over that initial onslaught of feeling. D.G. James points out that "[m]ere emotion in itself is something and nothing; what is necessary for poetry is the imaginative command of ... emotion.... There must go on a certain depersonalization, a quietness in the midst of the speed

> We've all heard the cliché, that "a picture is worth a thousand words"; a poetry though tries to make pictures with words, and helps us consider new visuals to create and clarify our thoughts and feelings. In his introduction to *The Imagist Poem*, William Pratt notes how "[i]n the poetic use of words, language is restored to communicative power, by being infused with new images.... It is the visual content of language then that makes it communicative, and it is the visual accuracy of poetry which makes it more communicative than prose." Poems use the image to engage our senses so that what we, as readers, experience is not just the expression of feelings/ideas but rather a means to reenact them ourselves.

of passion" (114).

It is from the 'balance of those opposites' from which poetry is born. "Hence, in lyrical poetry what is conveyed is not mere emotion, but the imaginative pre-hension of emotional states" (Preminger and Brogan 715). To put it another way, the per-sonal lyric poem is the reimagined casting of the emotion, designed to not only express yourself, but also to allow a reader to share the emotional state. That's why we study poetry. That's why it's an art.

> Here's a quick exercise on the lyric and metaphor. At its most basic, the per-sonal lyric is an expression of how we feel at the moment. So, using an image-based metaphor, write down the answer to "How do I feel?" *I feel like the plate glass window after the vandal left,* is much more memorable than *I feel sad*. Ditto, *I'm a cat stretched out on a patch of sunlight,* is much more effective than I'm happy.

Lyric poems may use elements of story, but their focus isn't on telling us a story; rather, personal lyric poems are designed to get us to think about the intense moments. When talking about short stories, we often say they end with an "epiphany," a moment of understanding or realization—you might consider the lyric poem to be pure epiphany.

Here's a contemporary personal lyric poem by M.L. Williams, that engages much of what we've been talking about.

Hat (2015)

In memory of my brother.

Artichoke leather, wide brim to keep
Coos Bay rain off the face, or sun,
no roll, slim braided leather bond,
your sweat still stains the band,
pinch slight and the crown flat,
a solid hat, something to wear
salmon season pulling kings
out of the Coquille to smoke

and grill to relieve the stress
of work trimming firs.
Spurred and harnessed, you hung
clipped to lines up a hundred feet,
watched the grounded world as a hawk
might till you were hung out
by a boss who hated your union line.
I hold it in my hand, but can't
put it on after you put that bullet
in your own beloved head.
Smell of leather, cigarettes,
what I have of you to hold.
I can't put it on.

This isn't really a narrative because there's no "story" per se, although there are hints of one, just enough to make us share in the anguish of the poet's loss. The glimpses we have of the brother function as a kind of montage: we have to fill in the blanks to make any story happen.

The hat becomes a metaphor for the grief the speaker feels about the loss of his brother. We know this just by the epigraph, "In memory of my brother," but the poet knows things the reader doesn't know: the particulars of *how* the brother died. Consider Williams's strategy of withholding the information about the brother's suicide—what affect does that have on the reader? Why might the poet hold off on letting us know this? Perhaps it is a fact the speaker wants to deny, a fact he doesn't want to face.

The poem begins with a description of the hat, the first line breaking on "to keep." In the sentence, the phrase continues on the next line with "Coos Bay rain off the face," but by breaking that phrase up with the line break, we also get another sense of "to keep," emphasizing not just possession, but an unwillingness to part with the hat.

Look at how maintaining our focus on the hat, Williams creates a different kind of suspense than if it were a narrative. The hat has a wide brim designed to keep the rain and sun off of the brother, but by focusing on the hat, the hat also keeps the fact of the suicide off of the reader for the time being.

More information about the hat moves the metaphor into the realm of synecdoche (in which the part is representative of the whole): it is "a solid hat," much like the speaker considers the brother to be. Look at the information the speaker gives us about his brother: he fished salmon, trimmed trees for a living, and who was fired for being a union activist ("hung out/ by a boss who hated your union line"). The brother is compared to a hawk, which is a proud, strong bird. The reference of the hat's "crown" and the "king" salmon associate the brother with nobility, a subtle sense of how the speaker feels about his brother.

The repetition of "can't put it on" has multiple implications: it captures the speaker's reluctance to accept his brother's suicide, but it also is a memorial to the brother, a headstone of sorts, something that keeps the speaker alive, imbued as it is with the scents and sweat of the brother's living.

On a sonic level, the poem avoids jarring sounds in order to give the poem a hushed tone (notice, for instance, how the brother trimmed "firs" which internally rhymes with "spurred" in the next line; "pines," although it would rhyme with "union line" later on, with its plosive opening would jar the softness of the shape of our mouth created by "firs"; although "conifers"—another word for evergreens—would work similarly to "firs," it doesn't feel like a word the brother would use). This is furthered by the fact that the first sentence works its way to the halfway point of the poem, giving the poem a sense of reverie. The poem's sentences become much shorter after the revelation that his death was by suicide, emphasizing the cutting short of a life, the shock of it.

So what are the hallmarks of the personal lyric poem?

- They use the I: there's a speaker present in the poem.
- They use imagery as metaphors for emotional/spiritual/ psychological revelation.
- They hint at story but don't tell a story.
- They have a musical component—their sounds (word choice, syllable, etc) help make meaning.
- They "hold a moment"; in other words, they're fixed on one event, one experience, and how it resonates.
- They are relatively short, often under 20 lines and many are less

than half that.

Things to Think about When Reading Personal Lyric Poems

One of the most important things to remember when writing and editing your own poems is the experience of the reader. Poems teach us how to read them, so it might help us to consider how to read a personal lyric. Remember, the lyric is about image, musicality and the intense moment. Like all poems, we come to them looking for the poet to guide us. We see things immediately, before we even read a word, that inform us how to read it: the line length, the stanzaic structure, the shape of the poem. Then we engage the tone of the language, the sounds of the words, the rhetorical stance toward the subject matter.

Here are some things to ask as we read such lyric poems. This isn't meant to be comprehensive, and you might brainstorm some other things you feel are important; the following questions are just meant to guide you when thinking about the personal lyric:

1. What is the "lyric moment" of the poem? Is it an emotional experience? A spiritual one? In other words, what is the poem about? Why do you believe this to be the case? How does the title help us understand the poem?
2. What are the central images of the poem? How does it/do they work? Are they surprising? Familiar? If familiar, is it used in a surprising way?
3. What is the structure of the poem—line and stanza? What words are highlighted by being end words? Are there any lines making meaning? Does the stanza patterning add anything to the meaning of the poem?
4. Are there any words in the poem that stand out? Which ones? Why?
5. Does the poet use any symbols or allusions in the poem? What do these add?
6. What are the key sounds in the poem, both vowel and consonant sounds? What mood do these sounds evoke?

With these questions in mind, let's look at a personal lyric poem together in order to put this basic reading into practice. Here's a poem by Christine Garren from her book, *Among the Monarchs.*

The Ruins (2000)

I think I spent my life
lying in the grass, waiting to be touched. And then I was

briefly held. And then I was left alone.

The rest of my life is a matter of return
to being with the wind, with a few lifting moths, the grass,

to the time before

I had felt any passion. —In the summer, in the past,
I would visit and tour the ruins of ancient cities.

Now there's no need,
the dust flown bits, the broken steps are in me—their clouds

of brevity and endurance.

1. The poem seems to be about a moment of understanding, of accepting one's loss in a relationship. Line 3 in particular seems to suggest this in which the speaker acknowledges that she had been "briefly held. And then I was left alone." The one line stanza after the initial couplet (two line stanza) seems to acknowledge her sense of aloneness.
2. The ruins of the title is the central image; they work as a metaphor for how she feels: abandoned, falling apart, but not "dead." As a matter of fact, people visit these ruins. Look how the poem ends on "endurance," which ultimately is a hopeful thought. Yes, civilizations are brief, love is brief, *but* we endure.
3. The lack of a set stanza pattern seems to enact her sense of fracture—she is in disarray emotionally. The use of couplets and single line stanzas suggest the difficulties of a relationship and the loneliness she currently feels, a sense of being "uncoupled." Meanwhile, the last words of certain lines stand out: "was" at the end of line two suggests a "death," a past tense of being, like

ruins once were. "Alone" stands out as the central emotion of the poem. Perhaps "before" sets us up for the final image of the ruins, something reaffirmed by "past" a few lines further down. "No need" establishes the strength she is trying to find in this being alone—to be the ruins, beautiful, resilient.

4. The first words create so much energy: "I think" shrouds the entire poems in uncertainty. Add to it the use of "moths" a word that echoes the word "mouths," which emphasizes the sensuality of love/desire. The key words at the end, "brevity and endurance" close the metaphor by emphasizing what ruins really are: a symbol of the brevity of a culture while simultaneously being an enduring artifact of that culture.
5. Grass is a very pastoral image, and although the poem doesn't give us a time of the year, the moths and the grass made me think spring, perhaps late spring, but not summer. Why is this important? Spring is a time of rebirth. She is finding strength in her new life.
6. Sounds in this poem don't necessarily do much in terms of emphasis or tension building. Early on the I sound dominates the poem, seeming to highlight the solitary nature of the speaker's hurt—her sense of alone-ness. The "-as" sound has some play in the middle of the poem ("grass", "past", "passion"). At the end the E sound stands out some ("cities," "need," "me," and "brevity") as does the N sound, which allows for a sonic continuity at the poem's end.

A Collection of Personal Lyric Poems

What follows is a collection of personal lyric poems from a variety of times and cultures in order to establish the ubiquity of the lyric poem and to provide an understanding of its development. Consider how the look of each poem sets up our expectations, and ask how the poem teaches us how to read it. Remember the list of questions posited earlier.

The Other Woman (2012)

— Kimberly L. Becker

I wake to blood-bloomed eye,
    broken vessel,
vivid vestige of a violent dream

    Why not?
Dreams are not some passive passage
There we war and also find the solace of our soul

This carnadine blossom in porcelain white
cries, *See? I vision past*
    what you can see mere waking

It was a tough fight
    but we won with a hard right
cross and you should see the other, knockout, woman

Fin (2010)

- Wyn Cooper

The stars are spare tonight—
a line strung across the sky
like buoys in the water
that show how close to shore
to sail and not hit rock.

I never thought it would come
to this, your cry on the phone
brittle as November ice, the way
you slammed the receiver down
without a human sound.

When I find our big bed
it's almost light. The stars
have fallen onto the sheets,
fallen down to sleep with me.

August (2000)

– Kathy Fagan

Because when rain falls finally
everything strains either into it or away.
Nestlings sway with their well-mouths
open and trees say Talk to the hand,
flipping their leaves up. Because when
the rain falls finally it hurts them a little,
like touch after none, like the moment
you know will not last that does last,
and lasts and lasts and lasts and then—
when exactly did he grow so thin
and why and who decided? Because
when rain falls finally the pond
must give up its silver, the windshield
its flash, and the black swan's orange
bill become the only value in the dark.
You glide by. It glides by. People are
sadder or less sad, depending.
Bougainvillea petals heap at curbsides.
And the whole world, which will never again be
without him, tilts south a little.
Why shouldn't it?

Woman Waiting (2015)

–Allison Joseph

I'm waiting in the airport
    for the hour of redemption
    heavy baggage for the journey
        weighting me at the wrists
I'm waiting in the train station
    for a minute of consolation
    watching arrivals and departures
        with a tattered schedule
I'm waiting in the supermarket

for a fraction of compassion
briefest eye contact
exchanged for my change
I'm waiting in the hospital
for a sliver of insight
all those numbers on my chart
some headache I can't read
I'm waiting in the bus depot
for a diagram of empathy
some chart of all the routes
to make a clean escape
I'm waiting in the alleyway
for a gram of grace
some bit of exaltation
to keep me from my own throat
I'm waiting in the settlement
for a flask of fantasy
some deep draught
I cannot help choke down
I'm waiting in the bathroom
for an inch of lucidity
some scrap of rest
unknown to any mirror
I'm waiting in the orchard
for a jigger of gratitude
some split of land unfettered
by the bruises of weather
I'm waiting in the graveyard
for a flash, a siren, a signal,
for confirmation this world
is more than anticipation
more than this mourning
collapsing and unraveling
never adding up
to any proper weave

Venus Transiens (1915)
- Amy Lowell

Tell me,
Was Venus more beautiful
Than you are,
When she topped
The crinkled waves,
Drifting shoreward
On her plaited shell?
Was Botticelli's vision
Fairer than mine;
And were the painted rosebuds
He tossed his lady
Of better worth
Than the words I blow about you
To cover your too great loveliness
As with a gauze
Of misted silver?

For me,
You stand poised
In the blue and buoyant air,
Cinctured by bright winds,
Treading the sunlight.
And the waves which precede you
Ripple and stir
The sands at my feet.

Fragment 168B (c. 590 BCE)
- Sappho *trans. by Diane Rayor*

The Moon and the Pleiades have set —
half the night is gone.
Time passes.
I sleep alone.

From Love, Imagination (2010)

– Sarah Sarai

As many bridges as I can walk
I have, suspended over

water's bounded body,
a bent-limb river flowing

in imitation of life's farewells.
Over opaline bowls and

chipped basins where nets
are cast so fathers and sons

can feed the hungry and
holy daughters work mysteries

of bounty: We are flesh and
gifted sustenance.

Along a roadbed I lose myself in
elemental apocalypse,

earth water air—and fire rushing
over the rumble spilling from

a reedy source to
a greater body demanding tribute.

Lipstick (1996)

– Jane Satterfield

Docs like dad's standard-issue dress shoes, combat
boots with zip-laces to accelerate the kill;

the leather jacket, the Joey Ramone.

Going to clubs in second-hand clothes,

bodies starved to sticks;
black liner, animal eyes, as if

to take back restless glances,
the desire to see and be seen...

In photographs from the '50's, the action painters'
wives are decked out, living dolls, the men self-important,

otherwise engaged. To hell with the beauty of easy
    equations—
creeps, criminals, flasher among the stacks—I'm talking

the flip side, damage we did: closed hearts, open legs.
The first fight I had with a lover ended in fists,

the blood left there till it flaked. Burning with boredom,
we wanted the ugly out in the open....

Destroyer, Great Mother, let me lay it on thick,
the shades I still own, blue-black as the bruise

left there, thick marks
like blood welling up.

Green Ash, Red Maple, Black Gum (1997)

—Michael Waters

How often the names of trees consoled me,
how I would repeat to myself *green ash*
while the marriage smoldered in the not-talking,
red maple when the less-than-tenderness flashed,
then *black gum, black gum* as I lay next to you
in the not-sleeping, in the not-lovemaking.

Those days I tramped the morass of the preserve,
ancient ash smudging shadows on stagnant pools,
the few wintry souls skulking abandoned wharves.
In my notebook I copied plaques
screwed to bark, sketching the trunks's scission,
a minor Audubon bearing loneliness like a rucksack.

And did the trees assume a deeper silence?
Did their gravity and burl and centuries-old patience
dignify this country, our sorrow?

So as I lay there, the roof bursting with invisible
branches, the darkness doubling in their shade,
the accusations turning truths in the not-loving,
green ash, red maple, black gum, I prayed,
in the never-been-faithful, in the don't-touch-me,
in the can't-bear-it-any-longer,
black gum, black gum, black gum.

I Wandered Lonely as a Cloud (1804)
— William Wordsworth

I wandered lonely as a cloud
That floats on high o'er vales and hills,
When all at once I saw a crowd,
A host, of golden daffodils;
Beside the lake, beneath the trees,
Fluttering and dancing in the breeze.

Continuous as the stars that shine
And twinkle on the milky way,
They stretched in never-ending line
Along the margin of a bay:
Ten thousand saw I at a glance,
Tossing their heads in sprightly dance.

The waves beside them danced; but they

Out-did the sparkling waves in glee:
A poet could not but be gay,
In such a jocund company:
I gazed—and gazed—but little thought
What wealth the show to me had brought:

For oft, when on my couch I lie
In vacant or in pensive mood,
They flash upon that inward eye
Which is the bliss of solitude;
And then my heart with pleasure fills,
And dances with the daffodils.

Some Writing Prompts for Personal Lyric Poems

1. Consider the textbox on the image and feeling on page 34. Now develop that idea further so that rather than a single sentence expression of a feeling, the metaphor is developed in a fully realized poem.

2. Look once again at Jane Satterfield's poem "Lipstick." Consider how the object is talismanic in the poem. Now think about an item from your past that has particular power for you. What was the source of its power? The context for its power? Write that.

3. Consider how Allison Joseph in "Woman Waiting" engages the notion of "waiting"and see how it feels the same in a variety of situations (the recurring lyric moment). See how she uses anaphora (incantation-like repetition at the start of each stanza) to help perpetuate the lyric experience. Write a poem using anaphora to enact the emotion of an event.

4. Look again at the sample poems and you'll notice how many of them engage aspects of the natural world as metaphor for feelings. Avoiding cliché, consider how the natural world might provide a description for a feeling. Use that as a starting or ending point for a poem.

Chapter Five B: On the Observational Lyric Poem

Not all lyric poems work on the premise of having an I who is doing the talking, who is addressing something about herself in some way. The observational lyric allows us to see through the eyes of the speaker (and hear through their ears, smell through their noses, etc.) in order to share the lyric experience un-mediated. Many of these poems are poems of witness: the poet is focusing on something observed. Like all American lyrics, such poems are characterized by the importance of a central image or set of images that help give concrete understanding to an abstract experience, and, although such poems were being written for generations, they came particularly in vogue in the wake of Imagism in the early twentieth century.

To help better distinguish between the personal lyric and the observational lyric, here are two poems by the American poet William Carlos Williams, the first a personal lyric.

The Young Housewife (1916)

At ten A.M. the young housewife
moves about in negligee behind
the wooden walls of her husband's house.
I pass solitary in my car.

Then again she comes to the curb
to call the ice-man, fish-man, and stands
shy, uncorseted, tucking in
stray ends of hair, and I compare her
to a fallen leaf.

The noiseless wheels of my car
rush with a crackling sound over
dried leaves as I bow and pass smiling.

Although this poem is chock full of observed material (what our speaker sees outside of his car), in the end, the poem is about his reaction to this vision; the poem is about what seeing this young woman does to him, and the lyric moment of the poem climaxes in the action of "I bow and pass smiling."

Consider how differently, then, a poem by the same poet operates, with the I removed, so that we experience the poem as an observation as opposed to a declaration.

Queen Anne's Lace (1921)

Her body is not so white as
anemony petals nor so smooth—nor
so remote a thing. It is a field
of the wild carrot taking
the field by force; the grass
does not raise above it.
Here is no question of whiteness,
white as can be, with a purple mole
at the center of each flower.
Each flower is a hand's span
of her whiteness. Wherever
his hand has lain there is
a tiny purple blemish. Each part
is a blossom under his touch
to which the fibres of her being
stem one by one, each to its end,
until the whole field is a
white desire, empty, a single stem,
a cluster, flower by flower,
a pious wish to whiteness gone over—
or nothing.

In "Queen Anne's Lace," the experience is the reader's to see, to experience for herself, without the commentary and attitude of the I getting in the way. Still, the poem maintains a perfectly lyrical sensibility. It portrays no story. It holds this fleeting moment for us to share.

The goal of the observational lyric poem is to engage the reader into an experience by presenting it "objectively." The goal is to make what is observed by the poet in the poem be observed by the reader when reading the poem. This asks the reader to invest imaginatively into what's being presented, to act as a witness to what the poem unfolds. Like all lyric poems, these are intense, often imagistic, and focused on the sorts of moments discussed earlier. Such poems remove the I from the poem, allowing the reader to become the speaker in some way.

As in all poems, word choice is important in an observational lyric; words convey not just meaning, but associative energy and attitude. They relate to other words in the poem both on a sonic level and in their ability to create related contextual and tonal sensibilities. Although observational, these poems are *not* objective: word choice influences and shapes how we experience what is presented in the poem.

The removal of the I from the lines of the poem does not mean, however, that the poem doesn't have personality. Everything from what you choose to witness to the words used to describe what is observed say something about your poetic vision. The American poet William Stafford in his fine essay "A Way of Writing" discusses how, in his process, he often starts a draft by looking out of the window and writing about what he sees. There is an abundance of possibility in this. Out of the window of my home office, I might choose to write about the pear tree, the neighbor's yard with its yipping dogs, skunks, the traffic on the main drag a bit further in the distance. Even saying "yipping dogs" has an attitudinal quality.

Here is a famous observational lyric written by Robert Frost; it borders on the notion of meditation, but its focus is on the current moment, the *now* of the third line.

The Need of Being Versed in Country Things (1920)

The house had gone to bring again
To the midnight sky a sunset glow.
Now the chimney was all of the house that stood,
Like a pistil after the petals go.

The barn opposed across the way,
That would have joined the house in flame
Had it been the will of the wind, was left
To bear forsaken the place's name.

No more it opened with all one end
For teams that came by the stony road
To drum on the floor with scurrying hoofs
And brush the mow with the summer load.

The birds that came to it through the air
At broken windows flew out and in,
Their murmur more like the sigh we sigh
From too much dwelling on what has been.

Yet for them the lilac renewed its leaf,
And the aged elm, though touched with fire;
And the dry pump flung up an awkward arm;
And the fence post carried a strand of wire.

For them there was really nothing sad.
But though they rejoiced in the nest they kept,
One had to be versed in country things
Not to believe the phoebes wept.

Like all lyric poems, the observational lyric connects the abstract to the image. This poem is about the way nature feels no sadness at loss, how where fire was, new life grows. It does so with the imagistic presentation of what grows in the place, such as "the birds that came to it through the air/ at broken windows flew out and in" and "the lilac renewed its leaf,/ and the aged elm..."

Frost is no stranger to irony, and here the irony adds a bit of humor to supposed starkness of the observed tone. The fire gave "the midnight sky a sunset glow," so that darkness was lit up, but not with promise (that would be *sunrise*). He winks at us a bit when he mentions "the sigh we sigh/ From too much dwelling on what has been." And notice how the house burned down, so that all that remains is the chimney (he points it out in a line so clunky, the line like the chimney stands out), where the fire may have started. It stands "like a pistil after the petals go": the pistil is the male sex organ of flowers, and so rebirth is implicit even in loss. By using this simile, too, Frost manifests the natural rebirth (as opposed to the building of a new house).

Compare this poem to Christine Garren's "The Ruins" earlier. The emotional center of this poem is not the I—it would be a very different poem if written in the voice of the person whose house burned down. Ditto, it would be a very different poem if it were written in the voice of someone stumbling upon the house, seeing it, and musing on how nature filled in what had been there. Such a poem might be about the speaker's own loss in a very particular and personal way. Frost, rather, attempts to show us the universality of redemption, of the beautiful growing where there had been devastation.

The poem's formal principles, its use of rhymed quatrains (four-line stanzas) put a human shape on natural regrowth. Perhaps they echo the regimented fields and plowing of a farm (we know this was a farm from "the barn opposed across the way"); more to the point, Frost is keenly aware that this is a construction, a poem designed to help us make peace with loss. "Everything happens for a reason," the old saying goes, but most times it is up to us to find the reason in retrospect.

> One type of observational lyric poem is the poem of description, the poem that asks the reader to look at an item, to focus our attention on the object. Some "odes" (poems of praise) are these types of poems, and in general, the descriptive lyric asks us to see an item in a new light. Charles Simic's early career is filled with such descriptive observational poems, as is much of the imagist movement. For more on this, see chapter 11.

So what are the hallmarks of the observational lyric poem?

- There is no I in the poem, though some such poems will use the "you" or even a "we".
- They use imagery as metaphors for revelation and symbol, but

the focus isn't on "personal" disclosure.

- They are a glimpse of a story, and because the events occur outside of the speaker's being, they enact the mystery of not knowing.
- They have a musical component—their sounds (word choice, syllable, etc) help make meaning.
- They're fixed on one event, one experience, and present it so it resonates for the reader.
- They are relatively short.

Things to Think about When Reading Observational Lyric Poems

Like the personal lyric poem, the observational lyric engages us as readers through giving us a only a fragment. We're looking through a microscope or a binoculars to see something happen that is meant to resonate with us. As readers we have to ask questions of the poem in order to have a full experience; these questions are meant as a guide for you when thinking about the observational lyric poems you've been reading. We, of course, look at many of the same things that we look at in discussing the personal lyric.

1. What is the "lyric moment" of the poem? Is it an emotional experience? A spiritual one? In other words, what is the poem about? Why do you believe this to be the case? How does the title help us understand the poem?
2. What are the central images of the poem? How does it/do they work? Are they surprising? Familiar? If familiar, is it used in a surprising way?
3. How does word choice help focus/color our attitude toward this experience? How does the writer control the mood/tone of the poem so that we understand what he/she is saying?
4. What is the structure of the poem: line and stanza? What words are highlighted by being end words? Are there any lines making meaning? Do the stanza patterning add anything to the meaning of the poem?
5. Are there any words in the poem that stand out? Which ones?

Why?

6. Any symbols or allusions in the poem? What do these add?
7. What are the key sounds in the poem, both vowel and con-sonant sounds? What mood do these sounds evoke?

So let's put this sort of basic reading into practice. Here's a poem by Jo McDougall from her collection *Dirt.*

What We Need (1998)

It is just as well we do not see,
in the shadows behind the hasty tent
of the Allen Brothers Greatest Show,
Lola the Lion Tamer and the Great Valdini
in Nikes and jeans
sharing a tired cigarette
before she girds her wrists with glistening amulets
and snaps the tigers into rage,
before he adjusts the glimmering cummerbund
and makes from air
the white and trembling doves, the pair.

1. Part of this poem conjures the feeling found in this line from *The Wizard of Oz*: "pay no attention to the man behind the curtain." This is a poem that observes circus performers being "human" not magical. It is a moment of understanding: the poem starts "in the shadows" as these two share "a tired cigarette," but the poem ends on wonder: the appearance of the doves that are symbolic for these two circus people.
2. We get two different images of these two people (nice, right? Two people, two images of them, two doves—non-duality): in the first, they are perfectly human, in the other, she "snaps the tigers into rage" (look how the language of that enacts the magic show) while he "makes from air/ the white and trembling doves, the pair."
3. One of the things that McDougall does here is use the word "we"—forcing us to see these two. It's a rhetorical gesture that brings the reader into the experience of witness. She puts us there. We are an observer with her. And look how she controls

us with this opening line: "It is just as well we do not see," and then presenting us with a vision of it. She wants us to remember the truth about Lola and Valdini.

4. The single stanza of this poem reaffirms the sense that despite the two visions of these individuals, they are singular people. And it reminds us, then, that we all have a two good and bad, weak and strong, ordinary and extraordinary aspects. Non-duality: coins have heads and tails.
5. Consider the word "snaps" in this poem. It's an onomatopoeic word (it means what it sounds like), and the way it is used it makes it seem like she does this with a snap of her fingers. The adjective "tired" before cigarettes is particularly freighted: the people are tired, the cigarette is perhaps old and beaten up. Like the best adjectives in a poem, it is surprising (we don't think of cigarettes as getting "tired"), and it helps the modified noun be more symbolic in the poem.
6. "Doves" obviously are a symbol of peace. McDougall says we go to the circus to see the magic, it allows us to escape the ordinary. It brings us, literally at the end of the poem, peace in the form of the doves.
7. The poem uses a full end rhyme "air/pair" to close the poem. It brings a little "poetry magic" into this free verse, seemingly ordinary observation, emphasized by the change of syntax. There are a lot of other sounds in this poem that radiate: the M sounds at the second half of the poem, the internal half rhyme of "girds her wrists in glistening amulets" which is emphasized by the G sounds appearing before each rhymed word. And the L sounds in the names of the characters: "Lola the Lion Tamer and the Great Valdini" help reinforce their connection as a pairing.

A Collection of Observational Lyric Poems

What follows is a collection of observational lyrics from a variety of times and cultures in order to establish the ubiquity of the lyric poem and to provide a richer understanding of its development. Consider how the look of each poem sets up our expectations, and ask how the poem teaches us how to read it. Remember the list of questions posited earlier.

The Sea at Our Door (2006)
—Joel Allegretti
For My Mother, 1929-2005

a butterfly batted its flame-and-leopard wings
against the salt breeze, flickered
through the sea grass maze like a dyed paper
likeness of itself and witnessed this:

a dolphin at the end of her day languished ashore;
her flipper spaded the beach; her tail begged the foam;
mourned by starfish, who envied their namesakes
buttoned in the warm spread of sky—
(we all want the property of light)—she nuzzled
the sand while her child bleated from the shallows;

the elegy wind sang down her back and bowed
her dorsal fin like a viola; a halo of gulls wheeled
overhead; she drank in their bony cackles
as she surrendered to a part of the earth
she was never meant to know

night keeps its promise;
it comes to each of us; somewhere in the ocean's
twilight shushing was the memory, now as lost
as a drowned ship, of joyful pirouettes
against a gracious moon;

the butterfly alighted on the pedestal of her snout,
its stuttering wings rousing her grateful anticipation
that the blue sweep above was another sea;
close your eyes, the butterfly said, *it's good to close them.*

Untitled (c. 1669)
— Matsuo Bashō *Trans. by Peter Beilenson*

Twilight whippoorwill ...
 Whistle on,
 sweet deepener
of dark loneliness

Notes On Longing (2004)
— Tina Chang

It smells of after-rain tonight.
Duck bones, a wounded egg on rice.
On the corner, there is a shop
that makes keys, keys that open
human doors, doors that lead
to rooms that hold families
of four or seven who sit at a table.
There is a mother who brings
sizzling flounder of a wide platter
for the family whose ordinary
mouths have been made to sing.

Alzheimer's **(2012)**
— Wendy Chin-Tanner

as if childhood had not
died as
if the intervening
years had
not passed you by
giggling she
is peeking at
you through
the widening
lacuna signaling ship

to shore unmoored
but restored to
your own private
time her face the
face of your waking
hours mother's
milk gone
sour if you let it
be again
as it was between
you then what
would happen to
what happened
to what was
real or
true or
true what
would you do?

Hour of Dawn (2005)
— Oliver de la Paz

The light covers us with little tongues,
making us conscious of bad sheet texture.
We hold ourselves in contempt.

Our bodies coax a story sunrise
cannot disrupt as shade passes.

Then morning—we think only
of the honeysuckle, the cedar
the trembling aspen,
its bark, a sepulcher-white moment.

In the low dream we turn and break ... our bodies
rise and breathe.

The hour of dawn holds us still.
We still our lungs. Eyelids clench
facing the sun and we fade.

Our skins warmed away from dormancy,
gleam star-like and far.

We are gathered back into the things of this world
and turn away from the sore-red sun, moved
to deny who we will be when we are awakened.

Summer in the South (1903)

— Paul Laurence Dunbar

The Oriole sings in the greening grove
As if he were half-way waiting,
The rosebuds peep from their hoods of green,
Timid, and hesitating.
The rain comes down in a torrent sweep
And the nights smell warm and pinety,
The garden thrives, but the tender shoots
Are yellow-green and tiny.
Then a flash of sun on a waiting hill,
Streams laugh that erst were quiet,
The sky smiles down with a dazzling blue
And the woods run mad with riot.

Too Much Yes (2008)

—Joy Gaines Friedler

Where is that part of *no*
that forms at the mouth
so sure of itself

it can beat up the boys?

Laid down like a word,
a broken tree limb,
like a blackout.

Something lives at the end of *no*.
Something not like a flower,
but rather, like a moon.

Solid. Concrete. Immovable.

Las Vegas (2011)
— Evelyn Lau

Ghost of smoke in the hallways.
Sour stench in the woodwork, behind the gleam
of renovation, the bamboo wallpaper,
gilt mirrors, the bed sealed in its envelope
of laundered linens. A dubious history.

Fremont Street, second tier to the strip—
toothy showgirls in bedraggled tail-feathers,
pint-sized cartoon characters mugging for photos
and spare change. In the souvenir store a bear,
costume head tucked under his arm,
pays for a Red Bull and a fifth
of vodka. Sludge of spilled drinks underfoot,
a sticky river of sugar and slurry ice
glazing the first paved street of Vegas.

On stage a magician thrusts his arm,
his leg, his whole upper body
through a box of whirring steel blades
and half the audience wanders away,
suspecting a con. Nowhere for a tired tourist
to sit but at a slot machine, numb
to the jingle-jangle, the grind and swivel.

The girls of the Glitter Gulch boast banners
across their bare chests that shout "Humph!"
and "Indeed!", as if this was some other world,
fifty years ago. Above, an American rocket
burns across the electric sky,
thin canopy of twelve million lights
shooting for the moon.

From *Translated from the Night* #7 (1935)
— Jean-Joseph Rabearivelo *Trans. by Robert Ziller*

Ebb of the oceanic light.
The octopi, in their drivel,
blacken the sand
with their thick ink;
but countless little fish,
which resemble shells of silver,
not able to escape,
struggle therein:
they are taken with nets
stiffened by dark seaweed
that become lianas
and invade the cliffs of heaven.

Potpourri (1920)
— Lola Ridge

Do you remember
Honey-melon moon
Dripping thick sweet light
Where Canal Street saunters off by herself among quiet trees?
And the faint decayed patchouli—
Fragrance of New Orleans
Like a dead tube rose
Upheld in the warm air...
Miraculously whole.

The Noon Hour (1916)
— Carl Sandburg

She sits in the dust at the walls
And makes cigars,
Bending at the bench
With fingers wage-anxious,
Changing her sweat for the day's pay.

Now the noon hour has come,
And she leans with her bare arms
On the window-sill over the river,
Leans and feels at her throat
Cool-moving things out of the free open ways:

At her throat and eyes and nostrils
The touch and the blowing cool
Of great free ways beyond the walls.

Some Writing Prompts for Observational Lyric Poems

1. One of the many things that define us is our sense of place—our sense of a landscape which elicits a strong emotional response. Each of us have what Richard Hugo called a "triggering town" that is sacred ground for us. So think of a place or a time that resonates for you and write down all the sensory perceptions you associate with that particular place or time. (Imagine: my grandmother's kitchen—the smell of garlic and Dove soap, steam of boiling water, static big band radio, a dog barking, my grandfather's Marlboros, the taste of yeast in the air, the neighbors arguing in the next apartment, etc.).

(Or imagine: After work....)

(Or imagine: My first car....)

Try to get as many **particular** images as possible, and don't be afraid to mix sensory perceptions (the taste of yeast in the air or—better yet—the taste of neighbors arguing ....). Now write this poem so that we understand your attitude toward the place based on the sensory observations your present.

2. Consider the William Stafford way of looking out your window and jotting down the first thing that gets your attention. Now using your imagination, expound on the image. How does it relate to mood? Develop a poem based on this interplay between what was outside your window and your imagination, but keep it in the realm of the observed.

3. Take yourself and a notebook out to a place where a lot is happening—a coffee shop, a park on a nice day, an accident scene, a courthouse, a bar. Write down what you see, hear, taste, smell, feel. Connect these things to their surroundings and build a poem around this experience.

Of course, so much of the poem depends on *where* you choose to go, which will help dictate the moods and tensions of the poem. Why did you choose to be at such a place? Why are *we* there? How is that hinted at in the poem through word choice, etc?

4. Look at Joel Allegretti's poem "The Sea at Our Door"; notice, how although the poem is about the mother, the I is removed from the poem, so that what we have are a series of observations of this woman. We know the relationship thanks to the epigraph, but we are removed from an emotional connection to her. And still, one is forged through the details presented. Write a poem that engages someone for whom you have great feelings, and bring that person to life without "story" and without the I so that readers can experience his or her being too.

5. Explore the gesture of Oliver de la Paz's "Hour of Dawn": how does the use of the plural first person engage us as a fellow observer with the I? Now write a poem that takes a time of day (or of the year, or a season) and makes us part of the observational experience.

Chapter Six: On the Narrative Poem

One of the ways we pass on information is through the telling of stories. Historically, the narrative poem is one of the primary modes poetry. Verse dramas, *The Odyssey*, Dante's *Divine Comedy*, *Hiawatha* by Longfellow are all narrative poems. In our experiences in childhood, many of our earliest storybooks are written in verse: *The Cat in the Hat*, the works of Shel Silverstein, etc. (I won't mention how many students tell me their favorite poems are by either Dr. Seuss or Mr. Silverstein; needless to say, I spend much of my time lamenting how little poetry they know!) Other narrative poems many students know include Edgar Allan Poe's "The Raven" with its refrain of "nevermore" and its story (by a somewhat unhinged narrator) of a visit by the title bird, and the perennial "A Visit from St. Nicholas" by Clement Clarke Moore with it's famous beginning "T'was the night before Christmas ..."

Since the advent of the printing press and with it the rise of prose as the dominant means by which to tell stories, the use of the poem as solely a storytelling device has waned. That doesn't mean no one is writing narrative poems today; it just means that how we think of narrative in poetry has shifted some. Many poets tell stories through poetry, relying on the art form's immediacy and its attention to language and images to help propel the plot. Like all good stories, though, it's also important to make sure there's a point to what's being presented. In other words, the poem needs to be more than just an anecdote, and one way to do this, then, is to write the narrative toward a lyric moment.

But the narrative poem isn't a lyric poem; narrative poems *think* differently than lyric poems, and they tend to be longer than lyric poems. They drive down the page not in an associative way but in a linear way, moving from beginning to end. Therefore, we can talk about a narrative poem in much the same ways we talk about a short story. Besides having a rationale, a good story needs to have some conflict or tension that is resolved/relieved via the narrative of the poem, characters (a protagonist and antagonist) help, and a setting. As in many lyric poems, a first person speaker isn't unusual in a narrative poem. And just as we said before, that the lyric poem might be considered pure epiphany, it helps a narrative poem to have an epiphany, some lyric pay-off for the reader.

We also have to talk about it as a poem: its attention to language, how it uses the image and figurative expressions (particularly recurring images and extended metaphors), its sense of poetic structure, and its keen sense of music. Also, keep in mind the compressed nature of poetry. Beware saying too much—the relationship between the poet and reader is intimate, and the reader needs to do some work in order to feel engaged with the actions depicted on the page. That doesn't mean a narrative poem can't be long (although the word "epic" has fallen out of favor, the term "novel-

> The narrative poem is often longer than the lyric poem, and as such one of the ways it has to work as a poem is in its sounds. By looking at the sample poems, you'll see how poets like Tim Seibles and Ned Balbo use traditional forms to bring rhyme and sonic play into their poems. But all the poems show an attention to the sounds of language and the pacing of those sounds in their lines and sentences. Say the poems aloud and listen to how words manipulate our bodies and our breathing. For instance, in Jan Beatty's "Going Deep for Jesus," (next page) the boyfriend's name, Stush, sounds "soft" (rather than a name such as Nick, with its sharp vowel and its requirement that we close our mouths fully to say that hard K sound at the end). What tension does the sound of such a name make? When you read Beatty's poem, listen to how she emphasizes different consonant and vowel sounds. Just in the opening lines, we have the internal rhyme of *back*, *jack*et, and *tax*, as well as more repetition of the K sound in *biker*, *pocket*, and *check*. Such attention to the aural quality of words is crucial to bringing a poem—particularly a longer poem—to life.

in-verse" still pops up regularly); it just means that a poem should use language economically.

That being said, we also must remember that first person narratives, in particular, are driven by the voice of the poem's speaker, the narrating protagonist (more often than not), and so the poem also must allow for the nuances of a personal voice.

Jan Beatty is a contemporary poet who knows how to write a narrative. Her poems are musical and assertive, with lines that use enjambment to propel the reader down the page and into the experiences of the poem.

Going Deep for Jesus (2001)

Run to the street light, make a right
at the blue car, and go deep
— Sharan Watson

1981, I'm on the back of a cherry
red Kawasaki with my boyfriend Stush,
my biker jacket bought with a tax return
from a year of waiting tables, stuffed
in my pocket the bad check I wrote
to see Stevie Ray play the Decade.
Down Beck's Run we hit Carson, my cheek
resting on Stush's firm shoulder till
the ground rises up with the hulk of J&L
across the river, steel house that burns it all,
an up-against-the-wall-fuck, thick &
ripping, everything is smokestacks
& yellow blaze. We ride the river roads,
looking for deserted two-lanes,
newspapers stuffed under our leather
for warmth. I want to forget my name—
everything but the sharp lean into
the next turn, the cheap slap of the wind.
Stush brags about his water-cooled,
two-stroke engine, but I just want
the contact high of leather, metal,
and the slow burn of a few joints.
Past the bridges & bridges, we ride

away from our fast-food jobs and
run-down apartment, toward the smell
of the Ohio, its perpetual mire, the rotting
docks and lean-to's, to what we knew.
I knew the muscles in his back & his
low voice would make me come
back to my self. We stop near the bog
of the river's edge to have hard sex
on the ground, our jeans still on,
trying to shotgun a moment, to split open
our lives in the brilliant light until
we were the mills, we were the fire.
It was then I decided god and orgasm
were the same thing, that if Jesus
had an address, it would be a dark two-lane,
if god were here, she'd shove down
like a two-stroke in a rainstorm,
she'd let it fly.

Notice how the poem begins with action, *in media res* (in the middle of things): this is a poem, not prose; poems are about getting us in motion. To use a metaphor, they're about what happens in the air, not about taxiing to and from the terminal. We'll get enough back-story to understand why this story is important (they're broke, they work crummy jobs, they live in the ugliness) in the course of the poem. To make it more than just an anecdote, we need to know why the story is important.

Compared with the lyrics we looked at previously, the poem is quite long, and it is tightly crafted. If you say the poem aloud, you should be able to recognize its strong sonic qualities. Be-yond its aural attentiveness, the poem's structure, particularly its sense of line, is well thought out.

Narrative poems ought to have a good understanding of the line and keep in mind how the line is a measure of understanding in a poem as well as a unit of rhythm. We see the line with our eyes, but we hear the sentence with the voice in our mind's ear. How the visual and oral experiences of reading converge helps give the poem tension and meaning. For instance, a few lines before the couple stops for "hard sex," the speaker notes: "low voice would make me come." The line break here emphasizes the sexual: the low voice of Stush, of the motor cycle's engine, of the region itself all might make her come. It foreshadows the sex that happens a few lines later, but it's grounded on the sensual of the preceding lines. The whole poem has been sensually (sensorally) alive. Another line from this poem that stands out is "& yellow blaze. We ride the river roads." Notice how the fragments of two sentences fuse into the meaning of this one line. It is almost as if Stush and the speaker are "yellow blaze."

Beatty's poem, like most good narratives, leads us to some understanding. Here, the lyric epiphany has to do with finding an understanding of god's nature. Just as the great painter Caravaggio used prostitutes, street kids, beggars and young thieves to be his models for saints, so, too, Beatty finds a god in the "fast food jobs" and "run down apartments." Remember, it is easy to write prettily about the pretty, it is a lot more difficult to make the rundown pretty. And because the speaker having this revelation is a woman, god, too, is a woman.

Just as with short stories and novels, not all narrative poems are first-person narratives. Narrative poems can take on the imaginative realms of fiction, too. As with some stories (consider parables), some narrative poems function on the level of allegory, which is a symbolic narrative, a story whose function is its moral and its characters a representative of ideas. This poem, by mid-twentieth-century Turkish poet Ali Yüce (translated by Sinan Toprak and Gerry LaFemina) is representative of an allegorical narrative.

Feast (1962)

Mama mouse sets the table
and then calls her spouse, the kids,
and her invited guests
who arrive gasping, excited
by the cat meat on the menu.

They ate, drank and burped.
They piled aboard a carriage made of an old trap

pulled by a noble tabby.
Inside, they carried on with gusto
riding to the festival.

If you win the race, said
Papa mouse to his boy,
I'll reward you with cat meat.
If you marry me, said
the girl mouse to her lover,
you'll never thirst for cat milk.

Unlike Jan Beatty's poem, this story is rooted not in a world we recognize, but in the realm of symbols. It's story isn't developed but it's not a lyric poem: it has a storyline, characters, and dialogue. "Feast" harkens back to the tradition of fables and children's books.

So what are the hallmarks of narrative poems?

- First and foremost, story drives the poem.
- They often use lyricism to create epiphany or understanding for the reader.
- Image, metaphor, and extended metaphor may help hold the poem together.
- They are usually longer than lyric poems because the story often needs more time to unfold.
- They may use refrains, incantation, and other formal and/or sonic devices to help hold the poem together.
- Rather than holding moments, they string moments together to create a narrative arc.
- They have characters (antagonists and protagonists), and often use other tools of story (dialogue, etc.).
- They can be in first, second, or third person.

Things to Think about When Reading Narrative Poems

Most narrative poems announce themselves and their stories immediately. As with short stories, they often begin *in media ras*, and they use the techniques of poetry to control how we readers experience this story. Lyricism is often connected to the notion of epiphany, and it's useful to consider when and where in a narrative poem does temporal movement slow down or stop so that the camera of the narration is held.

What follows is a list of questions we can ask while reading these poems. They don't all have to be answered; this is just a guide for you when thinking about narrative poems you might encounter.

1. What is the "story" of the poem? What is the importance of the story? In other words, why is it being told? Is there a lyric moment/epiphany in the poem?
2. Why is this written as a poem? In other words, was writing this as a poem as opposed to a story a choice? How does it work as a poem?
3. What are the central images of the poem? How does it/do they work? Are they surprising? Familiar? If familiar, is it used in a surprising way?
4. What is the structure of the poem—line and stanza? What words are highlighted by being end words? Are there any lines making meaning? Do the stanza patterning add anything to the meaning of the poem?
5. Are there any symbols or allusions that you see? How do they work? What do they do to "deepen" the pool, so to speak, of the poem?
6. Are there any words in the poem that stand out? Which ones? Why?
7. What are the key sounds in the poem—vowel and consonant sounds? What mood do these sounds evoke?

Well, in order to think about this, let's look at this narrative poem by Bruce Weigl.

What Saves Us (1990)

We are wrapped around each other
in the back of my father's car parked
in the empty lot of the high school
of our failures, sweat on her neck
like oil. The next morning I would leave

for the war and I thought I had something
coming for that, I thought to myself
that I would not die never having
been inside her body. I lifted
her skirt above her waist like an umbrella
blown inside out by the storm. I pulled
her cotton panties up as high
as she could stand. I was on fire. Heaven
was in sight. We were drowning
on our tongues and I tried
to tear my pants off when she stopped
so suddenly we were surrounded
only by my shuddering
and by the school bells
grinding in the empty halls.
She reached to find something,
a silver crucifix on a silver chain,
the tiny savior's head
hanging, and stakes through his hands and his feet.
She put it around my neck and held me
so long my heart's black wings were calmed.
We are not always right
about what we think will save us.
I thought that dragging the angel down that night
would save me, but I carried the crucifix in my pocket
and rubbed it on my face and lips
nights the rockets roared in.
People die sometimes so near you,
you feel them struggling to cross over,
the deep untangling, of one body from another.

1. The poem tells the story of how one young man confronts his fears of going off to war by trying to sleep with his teen-aged girlfriend before leaving for Vietnam. Instead of sleeping together, though, the girl gives him a crucifix. The end of the poem deals with what the speaker learned from this experience. This is the poem's lyric moment, where the crucifix becomes the "salvation" for the speaker and in the

end, he discovers the similarities between the time with the girl in the car and with his fellow soldiers in a foxhole.

2. The poem takes advantage of line as a means of controlling the pace and breath of voice in a fascinating way. If we look down the right hand side of the poem, we'll notice that each line is enjambed—there is no end-stopped line—until she stops him. Consider how breathless the speaker and the girl are in the moment of their passion. They're racing toward something (at least in his mind), and the poem races downward, too. This is noteworthy insofar as in the second half of the poem (the point in which fear, hesitancy, and death enter the poem), the line breaks are more often than not end-stopped—lots of periods and commas. The poem enacts the hesitancy of the second half. Lastly, notice how the poem's final image mirrors the early image: the two ways bodies untangle.
3. This is, of course, subjective. "High school of our failures" is a wonderful image, for it tells us a lot about who these kids are (not good students, etc.) *and* it foreshadows his failure to sleep with her. The simile of the umbrella blown inside out by the storm is also compelling. They are sweaty, windblown; there is the storm of the coming war. Some other images, most notably "dragging the angel down" and "heaven was in sight," are both pretty familiar, and may seem less powerful in one regard, though one could argue that they capture the young, colloquial sensibility of the speaker as a counterpoint to who he is today.
4. I've answered much of this in answer 2 above, but I think the idea that love and death are the two lessons here, that they are what makes us whole. The poem, then emphasizes nonduality—home and 'Nam, love and death: they're part of what makes us whole.
5. The biggest symbolic images have to do with "heaven" and the "angel" and the "crucifix." The crucifix, of course, represents Jesus. The girl in the poem remains chaste. The savior is the symbol of salvation, which "keeps" the speaker alive while he's in Vietnam. The religious imagery of the poem reinforces the power of the end.
6. The poem uses no surprising language; as a matter of fact, some

of the poem's strength is in the colloquial expressions and how they are used in concert with the other aspects of poetic craft. Weigl's skill is evident in how the poem moves between the surprising image *and* the commonplace—the ordinary nature of the outside school experience and the extraordinary nature of the rockets roaring in. The rockets, by the way, brought the *Star Spangled Banner* to mind, which is fitting in regards to the nature of the Vietnam War and a call for a particular type of patriotism.

7. One thing to notice about this poem is the S sounds: there are a lot of them. Since this poem is about a loss of innocence (not to sex but to the horrors of war), the S sounds, with their serpent-like hiss, bring the devil (from the Garden of Eden) into the poem, emphasizing the loss of innocence.

A Collection of Narrative Poems

What follows is a collection of narrative poems from a variety of times and cultures in order to establish the ubiquity of the lyric poem and to provide a richer understanding of its development. Consider how the look of each poem sets up our expectations, and ask how the poem teaches us how to read it. Remember the list of questions posited earlier.

Elizabeth and Elaine[1] (1997)
— Ned Balbo

Summer, 1967

I shook off the drops, and looked for my mother.
Elizabeth, glancing toward the deep end of the pool,
edged close to her younger sister. Elaine kicked water,
dangling her feet. Lance swam past, split the sun
in two, as Elizabeth laughed and shouted, "Dive!"—

[1] This poem is a sestina. For more on the sestina and other fixed forms, see appendix 4.

tossing up coins. Blue sky, reflected clouds

That shattered instantly. I kicked through clouds
still rumbling, but Lance was older, faster. Our mothers
watched us streaming with water from our dives.
Elizabeth's jaw drew tight—this was *her* pool.
Lance offered the coins; she took them. Would her son
surface just once, fists filled with coins, not water?

"Go!" She threw them to my side of the water.
I shot from the chrome steps, swam as if clouds
broke open inside my lungs, a dozen suns
sparkling before my eyes. I headed toward mother-
of-pearl, vision blurred, polished floor of a pool
still spattered with change, falling short as I dived

for nothing—a coin or two. Lance rose, every dive
triumphant. Elizabeth stared at the water,
waves displaced by his weight. I was tired of the pool.
Elaine twisted the strap of her suit, face clouded,
Her sister circling tensely—*I'm his mother*—
Elaine looked away, caught watching her sons,

first Lance, then me: *How could I give him away?* The sun
touched her bright hair, almost dry... Only one more dive,
one chance to prove who was the better mother.
I gulped air; the light dimmed. It was cold in the water
where loose change, falling, glittered through clouds
that scattered as all turned calm... The clear light of the pool

exploded. Submerged, I looked up: just a game of pool,
Lance banking from wall to wall, the firstborn son
slammed his fist on my chest, reached further through clouds
that tore as I choked and surfaced. Another failed dive.
I coughed, fought back tears, and dropped underwater—
Elaine whispered, "When will you tell him I'm his
    mother?"—

as I bounced, weightless in silence. A mother's
face rippled—I didn't want to come up, or breathe—and a cloud
of gnats touched the surface of the water.

Winter and War on Lake Monona (2004)
— Aliki Barnstone

I call my dear friend Edwin Honig
because winter is a burden to me.
It is like an ice block on each shoulder,
all the muscles tightening around my heart.

He says his college days in Madison
almost took his manhood. We laugh.
And he advises I buy a few pink
light bulbs to shed warm light around me

and start a story about our phone call
in which the student who read a newspaper
in my class is the same one I discover
fishing in an ice hut on Lake Monona.

Then I will have started a splendid event.
Indeed, who is this boy-man
who follows world affairs in spite of me
and my books? He sits alone

on the ice with a bottle of vodka
and he reads that yesterday the Iraqis
bombed Tel Aviv, the coalition forces
destroyed a hydro-electric plant

and a factory that, depending on who's
reporting, manufactures baby formula
or biological weapons. It is so cold
that we look at each other with tears

in our eyes. I think how tough he is,
patiently drinking as he guards the hole
in the ice, as his father and uncles did.
Every few minutes we hear warnings

on the weather channel: prolonged exposure
to cold can lead to irrational thinking
and death. Yet here he does for sport
what before was done for survival,

as if one could be impervious to the elements.
"Good boy, good boy, good boy,"
my student says as he bends to pet my dog.
What will *this* man do? He shows me pictures

of tortured POWs. I show him the box
of pink light bulbs I've bought.
Then we stand together a little embarrassed,
the tears freezing on our cheeks.

I carry home my fragile load,
and when I turn on the lights
—oh, splendid event!—
the walls are warm like flesh.

City of Tonawanda Softball Championship (2007)

— Sarah Freligh

Two down, two out, two on in the ninth
when Sid Szymanski stands in at catcher,
sorry substitute for Larry whose sure
hands were summoned to a plumbing
emergency by his buzzing pager in the bottom
of the sixth. Still, the usual chatter
Hum baby, hey baby hum hey Sidder Sidder Sidder
though Zack's guys are mentally packing
bats in bags, unlacing shoes in order

to get away—fast—before the Panthers,
arrogant bastards, can gather at home plate
in a love knot of high fives and beer foam
and gloat. Strike two and Sid calls time,
steps out to take a couple of practice cuts
a la Barry Bonds, like him a big man,
all head and chest, and *Siddersiddersidder*
the car keys are out, that's all she wrote
when the pitcher gets cute with a breaking ball,
hanging it a nanosecond too long, time
enough for even fat sad Sid to get around
and give that pill a ride.

Rounding first, already red faced, a crowd
in his throat, Sid wants to believe
it's not the sludge of a million
French fries, but pleasure
more exquisite than the first breast
he touched one winter Sunday
while his dad in the den upstairs
cursed the Packers and Bart Starr, while his mom
chattered on the phone to her friend
Thelma about the macaroni casserole
and menstrual cramps, Sid swallowed
hard and bookmarked his place
in *Our Country's History*, the page before
the Marines stormed the hill at Iwo Jima
and turned back the godless Japs, a high tide
clogging his chest as Alice Evans unfastened
the pearl buttons of her white blouse
and presented him with the wrapped gift
of her breasts, now second base and third
and the thicket of hand-slaps all the way
home where Sid hugs the center fielder
hurried and embarrassed the way men do,
oh, the moment, replayed again and again
over Labatt's at Zack's, the first pitcher
delivered by the great Zack himself

rumored to have been the swiftest,
niftiest shortstop on the Cardinal farm
but called to serve in Korea and after that
the closest he got to baseball was standing
next to Ted Williams at a Las Vegas urinal

Tomorrow Zack will make a place
for the trophy between dusty bottles
of Galliano and Kahlua while Sid
will field calls from customers complaining
about rising cable rates and too many queers
on TV, pretty much what he'll be doing
five years from now and ten when his wife
leaves a meatloaf in the freezer and runs off
with Larry the plumber and in twenty years,
when Zack's Bar is bulldozed
to make way for a Wal-Mart,
Sid will slump in a wheelchair
in a hallway littered with old men
mumbling and lost, wrapped
in the soft cloth of memory:
The arc of the white ball, a pearl
in the jewel box of twilight sky.

Painted Fire (2007)

—Jennifer Kwon Dobbs

Ohwon copied "Party by the Lotus Pond"
Locked in his employer's brass-hinged cabinet,

Which he polished everyday with root oil

except once when someone forgot to latch it
& Ohwon could not resist

opening the doors a little more.

So identical his version tht the yangban accused him
    first of theft, then of genius

not befitting an orphan drifter who didn't know his age.

Rumor summoned him to a springtime pavilion
    where the aristocrats gathered

ignoring the new kisaengs' raspberry wine.

The challenge, a poem composed for the event:

The vast earth and high mountains increase my will to fly.
Withered maples and falling leaves heighten my spirit.

He needed no outline, no bones for his eagle
    rapidly alighting from ink brush to paper,

feather by bristling feather as with searching
    for the thicker part of a branch.

The bird steadying its rippling weight above the vast
    empty field,

clutching & unclenching the phantom twig.
    A wash of ink leaves trembling

as Ohwon's bristles streaked clear, his body like the eagle
    circling the maple

to fasten roots to the rock face, then sitting on his knees
    as a twin appeared below

anchored & armed with a black-eye

The audience murmured among one another, how was this
possible?
He followed but broke Su Shih's aphorisms.

In Ohwon's one brushstroke, a thousand
transgressions & with each one, an increase in a will to fly!

Everyone Has a Story (2004)
— Erin Murphy

This is my grandmother's:
She is squeezed in the center of a convertible,
a 1934 Ford coupe, let's say—
red, like her mother's hair that whips
around in the passenger seat beside her.

The driver calls her mother *Vi*,
not *Viola*, and uses all the v words
he can muster. *My vivacious violet*,
he croons, then points to the Berkshires:
a verdant view. Asked if he's thirsty,
he answers with a deliberate very
as if it's the cleverest thing a man
has ever said. Her mother laughs,

the first sign, perhaps, of the looming
betrayal, like the girls who banish
one of their own, then giggle loudly
from swings across the schoolyard
to show the exiled one what she's missing.

Mr. Wey is how he's introduced
to my grandmother when he arrives
to take them for ice cream
and a drive in the country.
Surely not all the *gentlemen callers*
are villains straight from dime-store comics.

One, at least, must kneel down
to ask about her birthday
or to offer a teddy bear with a plaid bow
around its neck. Surely they don't all steer
with one beefy arm slung over the wheel
the way this man does as he winds
along the back roads of western Massachusetts
before cutting the engine
in front of a small brown house.
My grandmother is told to wait in the car.
Back in a jiff, her mother says
as Mr. Wey takes another swig
from the bottle in the paper bag
and tells her to decide what kind of ice cream
she'll get on the way home.

The story doesn't end when her mother
and the man stagger out and announce
they've just been married. It doesn't end
with the forgotten peach-flavored ice cream.
It doesn't end when my grandmother
tip-toes around him evenings
as her mother works split shifts
at the factory, or when, four years later,
he falls asleep in the green tweed chair
and never wakes up. It doesn't even end
with the small insurance check
that pays for her first pair of new school shoes.
When my grandmother learns years later
that Mr. Wey wasn't just another caller
but the real father she's never known,
the story is just beginning.

Richard Cory (1897)
— Edward Arlington Robinson

Whenever Richard Cory went down town,
We people on the pavement looked at him:

He was a gentleman from sole to crown,
Clean favored, and imperially slim.

And he was always quietly arrayed,
And he was always human when he talked;
But still he fluttered pulses when he said,
"Good-morning," and he glittered when he walked.

And he was rich—yes, richer than a king—
And admirably schooled in every grace:
In fine, we thought that he was everything
To make us wish that we were in his place.

So on we worked, and waited for the light,
And went without the meat, and cursed the bread;
And Richard Cory, one calm summer night,
Went home and put a bullet through his head.

Innocence (2002)
— Lee Ann Roripaugh

My parents wrapped an old sheet
around the playpen to shield me
from the television, but I learned
to pull up the edge and peer out
from underneath to see newsreels
from Vietnam. I remember stretchers,
helicopters, and trees flickering
sadness, ominous black and white.
But the night of the moon landing
I was given my dinner early
then plucked from slumber, flushed
and cranky, wrapped in a crocheted
afghan and propped up on the sofa
in front of Walter Cronkite.
I was four, and secretly I wondered
if I would see the moon rabbit,

who was pulled from flame and taken
to live in the sky by the old man
in the moon. But instead there was
crackling static, the disembodied
voices of the astronauts, chubby
in their white spacesuits
as they finally climbed down
the adder to bob on the rocky
surface of the moon as if it were
elastic as a trampoline. So quiet
and dark, it seemed lonelier
than Wyoming when snow spilled
over the fence tops and made strange
bent shapes of the Russian olive
and pine trees, hulking silent
humps of the car, and antelope
stepped into the frozen circle
of the city limits. I became
a child of the moon landing—
raised on Tang and Pillsbury space
food sticks chewy in the silver-
lined, tubular wrappers—my face
tilted up like a stargazer lily,
with its sick red-tipped matchstick
stamens yearning, antennae-like
for the Sea of Tranquility; the void
beyond. At night I watched the man
who lived in the house across
the back alley from my bedroom
walk around without his clothes
through my pirate's telescope.
And when I was tired of watching him
I watched the moon instead, hanging
pale orange, like a mellon-balled
scoop of cantaloupe in the sky.
Empty, shimmering rock-cold fruit,
but wanted to swallow it whole.

The Ballad of Sadie LaBabe (1992)
— Tim Seibles

Sadie LaBabe was a magic sister
Lord, even a blind man couldn'a missed'er
Her sultury skin was dark as shade
Her mind cut sharp as a butcher's blade
And the brothers who stared at Sadie's thighs
Would shake their heads and moan and try

'Cause Sadie moved like water poured
The shakes she shaped had angels floored
She knew her walk turned wind to fire
A wink from Sadie turned brains to mire

The mellow fellas tried to talk that sly
They'd high-sing "Sadie!" when she walked by
But if she stopped to pass some time
Their lines went stale and sank to slime
She yawned she'd heard it all before—
Stuff bad boys write on bathroom doors

'Cause Sadie pours like rivers move
Her black skin rocks men toward the blues
She won't be mine, she won't be yours
She bit Eve's apple down to the core

Now J.T. Kade was Billy-Dee handsome
His humble home they called *Love Mansion*
He was ice cream cool and built like a panther
Whatever the question J.T. was the answer.
The sisters crowned him King of The Land
He could make a girl faint just by holding her hand

So one fast day this last July
King Cool J.T. came boppin' by
Now Kade had come from way up in Philly
His eyes were steady, his lines were chilly

He said he'd come down Dallas way
For this heavy hittin' hammer they called LaBabe

'Cause Sadie loved like honey tasted
She'd groove you till your life was wasted
Her tongue was silk, her touch was satin
She'd soothe you till your hills would flatten

But Sadie Heard what the sisters said
About this brother who broke their bread
She made the pledge, "This Saturday night
I'll be home alone by candlelight
And if the Kade is whatch'all say
I won't mind much if he comes my way"

'Cause Sadie's heart could hold an ocean
she moved more ways than there was motion
Let tight be fat and tall be low
You gonna maybe-with-Sadie, she gonna stop your show

Three days went past and kept on goin'
By Saturday night a light breeze was blowin'
With candle-shine flecked in her eyes
Sadie sat lazy while the crickets cried
Her blouse was cotton, her shorts were suede
She had big doubts about this Kade

But from the porch there tapped a noise
And through the screen she caught his voice
"Say, Lady-Sadie, won'tcha let me in
I got some wine and some time to spend
I'm knockin' here 'cause I know you're there
Wanna slide my hands through your thick black hair"

So Sadie smiled and licked her lips
Said "*Greaze* and slide under since you're so slick
The pleasure's my treasure, we don't need no wine
I like your style and I've heard you're fine—

Let the body be danced and the soul be dazzled
Let's make love shapes till the stars get frazzled"

They talked awhile then he touched her face
She twined her arm around his waist
The chatting stopped, the kissing started
The routes they used had not been charted
They rocked the sofa, then bumped the door
They bruised the stairs, they warped the floor
The storm they raised blew out the candles
He held her hips like they had handles
A Whole day passed and neither seemed tired
If sex is electric this couple was wired

So Sunday went off when Monday morning came on
Sadie stood up and stretched, but Kade was gone
The grapevine say's he's in a home
For those who run where none should roam
They say he sings, he stutters, he raves
About some lady he calls LaBabe
For him the world has come unhinged—
He yells, "Sadie loves like a big fish swims!"
The doctors scratch their heads and frown
They drug his milk to calm him down

While Sadie sips soda by a swimmin' pool
Her mind is clear, her skin is cool
Sometimes she feels a little sadness
For drivin' Kade to that sweet madness
But Sadie holds what most let fall—
"*If you're gonna half-step don't step at all!*"

'Cause Sadie played in the Garden of Eden
She tamed the snake and taught him readin'
She won't be mine, she won't be yours
She ate Eve's apple and asked for more.

Some Writing Prompts for Narrative Poems

1. Imagine for a second that there was actually a Richard Cory or a Sadie LaBabe, whom Edward Arlington Robinson and Time Seibles knew or at least knew of. Now consider the people in your life. Maybe it's not someone you're close to, but just know of, know a little of his or her story. Write a narrative of that person. Feel free to use hyperbole, rhyme, and other aspects of poetry to bring the person to life.

2. Stories of initiation are an important part of the literary canon; our coming of age is rooted in the rites of passage that end in a variety of "first times." Think of a "first" in your life (without going for the obvious). Write the story of a first time event.

3. The stories we know best after our own stories are stories about our family—we've often heard them over and over, and their importance is known to us. Now look again at Ned Balbo's "Elizabeth and Elaine" and Erin Murphy's "Everyone has a Story." Write on of your relative's stories.

4. Reread Lee Ann Roripaugh's "Innocence." Consider an event from early childhood that might be explored through story and connect it to something else that happened later on in your life.

5. Lastly, the story of the quest, of being on the road, is a long standing trope. It comes with a starting point, a destination, and a rationale. Consider Jane Beatty's poem once again as a model, then write the story of a journey in the form of a poem.

Chapter Seven: On the Meditative Poem

In his second book, *Praise*, poet Robert Hass presents a poem titled "Meditation at Lagunitas." In it, Hass fuses a bit of narrative, with lyric observations, and a bit of his own thinking about "big picture" concerns. "All the new thinking is about loss" the poem begins, and we're set on a track to know that this isn't a lyric poem, nor is it a narrative. Instead, we're going to follow along with the poet's thoughts on a particular subject for awhile. We will assume what the poet assumes.

It's from the title "Meditation at Lagunitas" where the next poetic mode gets its name. Meditation not in the Buddhist sense, but rather in the sense of to think about something, to give something time and consideration, so that we might also call such poems contemplative. They may seem like "stream of consciousness," but they are more than just a loose set of associations; instead they are focused, connected by image, story, the poet's obsessions, language, and more.

Like all poems, the poetic meditation attempts to show the reader the process of a mind at work, and asks us to follow in the thinking. Often quite long, this poetic mode establishes connections between narrative fragments, lyric experience, word association, abstract thought, and images, and it considers how these sundry items are connected and why they may be important—literally trying to contextualize an understanding in the life of the speaker.

If you prefer, we might say that the poem is *musing*—considering or thinking about a subject poetically (as the root of that verb is *muse*, the goddess of poetic inspiration). Often these poems may come to define an abstraction or a belief, but the definition is always contextualized within the poem's lines, its universal implications are subjective. In other words, I might write in a meditative poem that "Anger is a type of light" and in the confines of the poem, its meaning is clear; it is hoped that how the meaning reveals itself within the poem reveals a similar application in the reader's experience. Therefore, the lyric experience is the coming wisdom of the poem itself, the epiphany developed in the process of meditating, and the lyric result becomes a part of our thinking as well as something we might feel.

The reader, after all, is going along for the ride, and by making associative, narrative, imagistic, and lyrical leaps along with the poem, the reader finds himself mimicking the poet's thinking. Remember, the poem is more than just abstraction linked to abstraction; as we said earlier, the image has to embody the idea, and story can give context for it. Just as the lyric poem tries to unfold the lyric event and the narrative may attempt to tell its story, the meditative poem attempts to think about the importance of a particular moment or set of moments that help create a moment of lyric insight.

To better understand the relationship between lyricism and meditation in a poem, let's look at this poem by Joseph Fasano.

Heraclitean (2012)

More than once I was saved by ruin,
cupping my face in its hands as its wild hair

filled up the pastures. I lie out on the margin
of the river, listening to the lost carry

the exquisite kestrels of their minds
into the shallows, drowning them like infants

in their feathers. Their thrashing is a small song.
More and more I am asking more of rapture.

Tonight I watch the dark flocks filling up
the acres, and I think of a man and woman

lying in a locked house in their country, their bodies
touched by the small comfort only evening can offer them.

I can say it, now: Their bodies are not twin cellos
that have played out their hollows to exhaustion.

Their language is not the sound of water
falling all night into itself while a moon, in her fixed

praise, watches. More than once I have stood
at their threshold while the wind took their secrets

away, the small lamp of their land's fruit
beside them. I see now

the body is not a story. I see now the makers
will absolve themselves of nothing, the poor

once touched by winter come to winter. I rise up
and walk down to the water

where the roots are. April now. Wide
is the river and its one song.

Dark stars, dark stars of whom I'm ashamed
and in which I cannot

believe, come out
as you have always come

out, in splendor. Tell me the world is not a history
of settled things, the lost ones in the drama

of what's over. Tell me the night is not
enough, the wind is not

the steady one
wading with these frail forms

through the river, to bring them into stasis,
its disaster. Tell me

it is quarrel's world, no
other, that we howl out with the lush

and loss forever, that the rest belongs to Fire, only Fire.

Just with its title, the poem informs us that it's in the meditative mode, which refers to the philosophy of Heraclitus (who gave us the notion that we can't step into the same river twice). If that's all we know about Heraclitus, we have enough to know: 1. The poem is a meditation—it's engaging philosophical ideas, and 2. Water is involved.

Still, there's more to Heraclitus than river water. He believed that the universe is a balance of opposing forces (consider how the couplets engage that sensibility, ditto the man and the woman later on) and how fire is the opposing element to water. Of course, a lot of readers might not know this about Herclitean philosophy, but like the best allusions, not getting it doesn't take away from the experience of the poem. One understands this poem even without any knowledge of Heraclitus. Why? Because the poem clearly portrays the speaker's thought process, so that even if we don't ask questions about the title, the first two lines engage us in meditation by presenting us with the abstraction of "ruin" and the personification of "its hands" and "its wild hair."

> An allusion is a reference to something else: a text, a painting, a film, philosophy, what have you. Allusions deepen the pool in which we swim, but the best allusions don't overwhelm the poem, but rather help clarify the poem. In the best work, a reader may not "get" an allusion but still understand the poem. Some poems, like T.S. Eliot's *The Waste Land* are overwhelmed by allusions, and because of that poem's fame, some novice writers believe filling a poem with references to obscure texts or art will make their poem stronger, but the risk is turning off readers and writing a poem that seems pretentious and self-indulgent.

The poem's first four stanzas exist in this realm of metaphor. It isn't until line 9 that the poem moves away from metaphoric thought into a narrative, beginning with "Tonight, I watch the dark flocks..." As readers, we're suddenly grounded with a character, a time, and a place. Such grounding allows us to enter the poem imaginatively.

It should be noted that poems are as much about what is said as what it withholds from the reader, and this is particularly true in the meditative poem. Poems can have secrets, but they can't be riddles. In "Heraclitean" we don't know *why* the speaker "think[s] of a man and woman//lying in a locked house in their country," but we can assume it has something to do with "ruin" early on. Tonally, the poem has established a mood that permeates how we read it. The speaker has experienced "ruin," and perhaps he recognizes himself in the relationship between the man and the woman—hinting, perhaps, that the ruin was the result of an end of a relationship. Whatever else, he won't experience the same ruin again (although other ruin, sure).

Notice what happens in the narrative parts of this poem. He states:

> ... More than once I have stood
> at their threshold while the wind took their secrets
>
> away, the small lamp of their land's fruit
> beside them.

If he's stood at the threshold of them, is he standing at the threshold of being in such a relationship? Or just watching from the outskirts? What happens? The wind takes their secrets away (another type of ruin), and we're left with the clause: "the small lamp." Do we read that as what's left for the couple, or is it metaphoric—the secrets were the small lamp? Or did the wind take those as well? Grammar is complicated, and it helps bring both clarity and ambiguity to a poem.

From there the poem changes direction and addresses the spiritual by addressing the "Dark stars": heavenly bodies one cannot see. He's looking for advice, for guidance, but by asking for the "dark stars" to tell him, by stating it, he already knows. He's come to a realization that "it's quarrel's world" which again hints at something about the relationship.

The poem then presents the poet's thought process on these matters and thus is representative of the meditative poem. In "Heraclitean," narrative, lyricism, abstract thought, pre-existing knowledge (Heraclitus), emotion (loss, love) and imaginative thinking all weave together to come to a moment of acceptance about the ways of the world. With it's associative logic and leaps, it feels like "stream of consciousness," but it's a crafted thing, edited to this focused sensibility.

Here are some hallmarks of the meditative poem:

- It's longish.
- It mixes narrative and lyricism with regards to the thought process, and it may use multiple narratives to make a point, the way when we tell a story other stories may come to mind.
- It often fuses narrative and lyricism with abstract thought, imaginative thinking, and other knowledge.
- It makes statements about big themes while knowing they are only truths for the poem.
- It connects the "now" of the poem with the personal past as well as with other stories/myths/legends, etc.
- It often ends on a startling image or idea.
- It sometimes defines a concept in the poem.

Things to Think about When Reading Meditative Poems

Whereas narrative poems often have a shorter line because their thinking and their drive are linear—this happened then this happened then this happened, the meditative poem follows the thoughts of the speaker as he or she meditates (or contemplates) something. As with most of our thinking, the meditative poem moves around—a story reminds us of the news, of something we saw a week ago, or an old friend. The notion is that these things run parallel in our thinking, and the meditative poem takes strands of these parallel threads and weaves them together to make a stronger rope. The movement between threads isn't "linear" but lateral (a kind of lane change). So think about these questions as you read your meditative poems.

1. Is there a logic to the poem's movement? Can you identify a main "story" of the poem? What are the secondary threads? Is there a "big issue" the speaker is meditating on? Does the poet ask any questions? What answers does he or she find?
2. Oftentimes, the meditation is on a lyric experience, as if the poet is trying to understand or contemplate or share with the reader the importance of a particular "moment." Is there a lyric moment/epiphany in the poem?
3. Why is this written as a poem? In other words, was writing this as a poem as opposed to an essay a choice? How does it work as a poem?
4. What are the central images of the poem? How do they work? Are they surprising? Familiar? If familiar, Are they used in a surprising way?
5. Are there any symbols or allusions that you recognize? How do they work? What do they do to "deepen" the pool, so to speak, of the poem?
6. What are the structural concerns of the poem's lines and stanzas? The line in meditations often might be "longer"; how do the lines work? Are there any lines making meaning on their own? Does the stanzaic patterning add anything to the meaning of the poem?
7. Does the poem use any abstract thinking? Outside knowledge? To what affect?
8. Are there any words in the poem that stand out? Which ones? Why?
9. What are the key sounds in the poem? What mood do these sounds evoke? Over the course of a longer poem, sound interaction might morph and change? To what affect?

Here's a fine poem by Thylias Moss that uses the meditative poetic mode.

Fisher Street (1988)

I like to walk down Fisher Street
Everybody hangs laundry in the backyard

most of it white and durable

I think of hundreds of gallons of bleach
zinc tubs, clothes stirred with sticks

Fels Naptha, water hot enough to dissolve skin

mortuary stillness forced on children during a sermon
the clerical collar stiff and sturdy as a blade

a rude white, too much contrast with his face. I look away

think of monks mashing grapes
staining their feet the blue-black of a man from Niger

I think they'll never get their feet clean

Chix diapers white as glory, so clean
they're cut into placemats or made into pillows

once the children are grown.

I think of graduation, colorless, odorless diamonds
yellow, white and black gold

I think of weddings, bachelors, spinsters, gigolos and hookers

I think of degrees, murder, justifiable homicide
the dead man's clothes hanging dry

pants pockets pulled out and exposed

shirts buttoned to the throat, sleeves at the wrist
all faded, white after so many washings. The widow's hair

Everything plain as day.

I want everybody listening to the same 24-hour station
everybody singing along till hoarse voices

make only whispers and prayers

Sing till it's cold out and the song rises like vapor,
the breath of winter, white and bleached

like all that laundry waving on the line, dancing to the song

struggling like all of us to be free.
I don't expect to see

any other angels.

1. The poem follows the thoughts the speaker has as she walks down Fisher Street, a block through a poorer neighborhood. As she walks, she thinks about old monks, of people in the neighborhood, of different futures for these people, and of their salvation in the form of the angels at the end.
2. The lyric experience of this poem is the experience of Fisher Street. She's capturing this moment, but the street stuff (the diapers on the line, for instance) disappear into the specific thoughts she is having. The poem ends on a positive: the notion that among all this profane stuff is the sacred of those very earthly "angels" that end the poem.
3. The poems uses all the compression of poetic writing. The poem uses a lot of sound play and some formal aspects to fullest advantage.
4. The poem has a lot of surprising images, made more surprising by the juxtaposition of certain words and phrases: "the clerical collar stiff and sturdy as a blade" surely makes us rethink the minister's collar—it's suddenly dangerous. And it reinforces our notion of this neighborhood. "I think of graduation, colorless odorless diamonds" shifts our thoughts from school commencement to the ranking of diamonds; and she uses a similar shift when she says "I think of degrees"—because of "graduation" earlier, we think school degrees, but instead we get "murder, justifiable homicide." This isn't a neighborhood where people graduate. Yet these people try, she points out with the surprising images of the diapers "so

clean/they're cut into placemats or made into pillows//once the children are grown." See how the poem runs a familiar image in a unique way; this poem is about sharing everyone's dirty laundry but only after it's been cleaned. The whole neighborhood is "exposed" but that's okay.

5. Well, the name of the street is Fisher Street, and the poem is about salvation. We have a minister in the poem, monks, and angels of the ordinary. Jesus, of course, invited the apostles to be "fishers of men"—and there's a reason why the "Jesus-fish" adorns the cars of many Christians. How does thinking of this symbolism help us read the poem?
6. The stanza structure with its 2 line/1 line alternating pattern seems to capture a walk, which is what she is doing. The lines, as they stretch out, follow the distance of walking. Look how many of the lines start with "I think" (Such repetition of opening phrases is called anaphora.) This creates a kind of incantation and repetitiveness that again mirrors the act of walking while also emphasizing the meditative qualities of the speaker. As with all repetition, she mixes it up because even a walking rhythm: she brings in the negative "I don't expect" which emphasizes the end of the walk and the end of the poem.
7. There isn't much outside knowledge or abstract thinking brought to bear in this poem, but the poem's associative leaps (the "degrees," the "graduation") surely reflect Moss bringing other information into the poem.
8. There are many key words in this poem: "exposed" and "free," in particular, stand out because this is a poem about being free.
9. Moss does some things beautifully. She moves between various moments of alliteration to give the poem an ever-changing ear that keeps the aural elements as surprising as the informational elements ("degrees...") and the more imagistic elements. Early on the ST sound is predominant: "street," "stillness," "sticks," "stirred," perhaps reminding us we're on a street. The A and E sounds both appear often then: E, with its siren-like cry and A with its positive connotations; perhaps this is deliberate, designed to remind

us that both the good and the bad co-habitate on this street—the ministers and the hookers both reside there. It's important to note that the final stressed vowel sound is the A in "angels" letting us "hear" the winning sound. I also like what she does with the P sound (she uses it a great deal) to almost tongue twister effect in this line: "pants pockets pulled out and exposed." It's a sound that pops, as it were, and after the homicide a few lines earlier, it brings out an almost popping effect, perhaps like gunshots.

A Collection of Meditative Poems

What follows is a collection of meditative poems in order to establish the ways such poems work. Consider how the look of each sets up our expectations, and ask how the poem teaches us how to read it. Remember the list of questions posited earlier.

Conviction (1991)
— Alice Anderson

When you talk yourself out of love you will have not only a sick feeling
deep inside your chest below the place your black bra holds your breasts

like he did, sometimes in the night, lifting them to moon-light, but you will be
so cold. You will wake up and the skin of your breasts will be cool to the touch

and your breath will be rough and short. You will not go back to sleep, not
without the tiny blue pills you have begun to keep on your bedside table.

When you talk yourself out of love you will get out quick, and you will be mean. You will write letters with a lot of *absolutely positively's* in them

and you will send the letters. You will throw a gold ring into a basket of trash
and you will write about the ring and the basket of trash and later, when you wake

in a sweat, you will get the gold ring out. When you talk yourself out of love
you will go out to bars and other, normal places, where everyone will become

a possibility. You will talk yourself into people who could be dangerous. Even
boring people will seem bearable. You will have a lot of unsafe sex. You will have

sex with your eyes closed and concentrate on remembering the name of the person
you are fucking. You will say the name over and over again until it sounds like nothing.

You will turn your head away from their kiss that tastes like salad oil and you will see
something gold glinting on the bedside table. You will reach your arm out to touch it.

You will touch the love you left in the darkness. You will touch yourself, for you
will be the only way back to the one you left. You will say the name of the one

you left out loud until it begins to sound like your own. You will put your fingers in
to fill your mouth with what you imagine is the skin you no longer get to touch.

And that taste will drown out every other taste. Baked bread will taste like him. Mint
gum will taste like him. You will cry out his name once more, and you will be surprised

when there is no answer. You will become quiet then. You will stop saying the names
of things you touch. When you talk yourself out of love it will take a while for you

to become numb to your own blind convictions. Talking yourself out of love is, after all,
what you are good at. You will talk yourself out of it all and you will feel sane and clean

and right. You will go to more bars and you will bring home only girls then and when they
say their names you will yawn in your head, closing off your ears, so that you will not

have to hear their names. You will make it through the sex and you will exhaust them
so that they will fall asleep in your bed and you will watch them sleep with their hair

on his pillow. You will kiss them while they sleep. You will touch the hair of a very
pretty brunette who looks nothing like the love you no longer have. You will bite her

fingernails. You will write your name on her forehead. You will tell yourself she is
beautiful. But she will never be beautiful enough. No one will be beautiful enough.

You will go back to the bar and find a man who is almost no ways beautiful, one who

will not sleep in your bed. And then, you will talk yourself
into him. You will decide

one day as you are taking your shower to love him. You will
love him. He will hit you
sometimes and you will love him. You will not run away
from this. You will not run away

from anything. He will shoot a gun once, yelling at you,
firing rounds into the ceiling.
You will not even flinch. He will beg you to leave and you
will not. You will not

leave the house. You will feel neither scared nor ashamed.
You will feel strong
and strange and human. You will talk yourself into this love.
It will be easy.

Thinking American (2000)

— Hayan Charara

For Dioniso D. Martínez

Take Detroit, where boys
are manufactured into men, where
you learn to think in American.
You speak to no one unless someone
speaks to you. Everyone is suspect:
baldheaded carriers from the post office;
old Polish ladies who swear
to Jesus, Joseph, and Mary;
your brother, especially your brother,
waiting in a long line for work.
There's always a flip side.
No matter what happens,
tomorrow is a day away,
or a gin bottle if you can't sleep,
and if you stopped drinking,

a pack of cigarettes. After that,
you're on your own, you pack up
and leave. You still call
the city beside the strait home.
Make no mistake, it's miserable.
After all, you bought a one-way
Greyhound ticket, cursed each
and every pothole on the road out.
But that's where you stood
before a mirror in the dark,
where you were too tired
to complain. You never go back.
Things could be worse. Maybe.
Detroit is a shithole, it's where
you were pulled from the womb
into the streets. Listen,
when I say Detroit, I mean any place.
By thinking American, I mean made.

Joyride In Blue (2014)
— Silvia Curbelo

What is lost, what is broken,
the sweet slide of two worlds
colliding into night. Call it
a journey, a geography,
tangle of wires and TV light,
the insomnia glow of boredom
that has you reaching for the car keys
one hundred miles from morning, bone—
tired white flag of 6 a.m.,
as you slip behind the wheel
with a radio wide open.
And the street like a face in every mirror,
pulling you out from that starting place
where home and motion intertwine,
steam on the shaving mirror, gold script

on the blue towel, *His*. Not his.
But this is not the stone you carry,
work boots and wanderlust, the clatter
and hum of being alive, full-ride nightscape
splashed across your windshield like the back hand
of forgiveness, a kind of loose rain in the weeds
and empty lots of L.A., past the sinewy
figures of love, ghost deals gone sour
and a song in every shot glass.
Let's call in the blues, barkeeps
and cabbies cashing in their fares
to head home before the day breaks open
with its backslide of regret.
But not yet, not this moment,
windows rolled down to whatever
wind flies in, slow grind of salt
and blue neon, past lit up
tenement windows, museums
of rust and moving on. And desire
like an afterthought, all flash
and blur, the last-ditch starlight
of ten thousand cigarettes going in the dark.

Vantage
— Laura Da'

Driving past Vantage:
          damp sign proclaiming ginkgo fossils
and iron sculpture of wild horses on the ridge.

At the turn of the last century,
Cayuse ponies were bred with European draft horses.
          A leaner, tougher work animal for the logging fields.
Trumpeter swans stitch
          the sallow slab of sky.
                Two birds swap point position
                                                to cut the air's polarity.

Path that pulls the taste
of mixed blood into my mouth.
Late February
and I am three weeks pregnant. I drive
        and the Columbia loosens
            my dad's easy silence.
He talks about his grandfather:
star musician of the Haskell Indian School Marching Band,
        telegraph operator, rodeo cowboy?
Tracking his family across
three states to hunt for big game
was habitual.

My grandfather,
dead within a week of my birth;
        I am told
            he looked at a Polaroid
            and proclaimed me an angry little Indian.

Late August in a post-depression labor camp
in the Mojave desert.
    My dad was born; he might have been premature,
        covered with dark hair and sick enough to die?

Terraced sun shower wading through the cloudbank.
        Recollection becomes embrace?

At twenty-nine weeks,
the doctor's chart advises me—
    my child is two and a half pounds, like a Chinese cabbage.
Blinking heavy eyes and fluttering his newly formed lashes.
My hair still damp from swimming laps.
        Warning signs:
    severe headaches, excessive nausea, a change in reflexes.
Feel of the doctor's hand pushing me back onto the table.

In the hospital, I ask for books.
        Posters from old rodeos.

A photo of a Mimbres pot
from southern New Mexico
black and white line figures—
        a woman dusting corn pollen over a baby's head
        during a naming ceremony.
Medieval women
        ingested apples
            with the skins incised with hymns and verses
as a portent against death in childbirth.

Heparin Sodium
injected daily and nightly
        in a slow abdominal arc
incising my skin
        like a creation spiral; my hope apple.

Say splitting the rails of the body
to lay down a fence
between harm and one's young.

Terraced sun shower wading through the cloudbank.
My son at ten months
staring calmly at morning stars
during his naming.
The faint trail of corn pollen suspended
        in his fine, dark hair.

Stupid Chicken Falls in Love (1991)
— Kate Knapp Johnson

Standing in the wrong
line at the check-out, cashier
screaming to the manager: "Void!
"I've got a void here ...," I have plenty
of time to scan headlines
in the racks. NATIONAL
ENQUIRER, STAR, WEEKLY WORLD full

of Elvis sightings, miracle
cancer cures, Carmelite
nun forced to make love to space
visitors, and this: Stupid
Chicken Falls In Love
With Pick-Up Truck.

I think I ought to be
above all this, our gumball
world, its schlock
and tack. I want disdain
enough to turn away—

but frankly all my life
I've turned away
from seeing what I am: expert
in the art of hedging, acting
like an "educated" person with a little

dough, some sort
of fucking privilege that shelters me,
makes me better, far
too cool to care
about nuns and loud cashiers, beyond belief
in Elvis or these shopping carts of whining
kids and melted fudgsicles ... Inside,

I'm runny as an egg, ashamed; afraid
you'll find me out, I hide
in self-help books that say:
I should assert, suspect, avoid
dependencies of any sort, look out
for numero uno, take care
of my needs, my
cholesterol, my lingerie—seriously,
who hasn't, just once, pretended
to be clean of earth, inviolable, a perfect
fartless speciman.

It doesn't matter what
wakes us, or when, so long as we do
wake and step
into our lives—here, in this supermarket
I stir, arouse, and see: one

Nebraska prairie chicken. White feathers
all fluffed out, air sac
on his neck inflated, he hoops and stamps—
a loaded diaper on two pocked legs—
this prairie courtship dance
every time the blue Dodge truck
comes home across the meadow. All night
the bird roosts inside the paneled cab, soft smell
of cows and plastic, far light
of stars ... While in the house the farmer lies
beside his cranky
comfortable wife, smiling, strangely attached

to this chicken who stoops so low
to love. What does this farmer in Nenzel
know? I stare
at the cashier, her tinted hair, mouth
snapping gum, eyes caked
with Maybelline. I stare at her to whom

I'm kin. Our skin and veins and genitals
connecting us, relatives
to bat and buffalo, iguana, antelope, house
cat, the man
who runs the heavy print machine, the secretary

with the twitch and I say here's
to it—what
connects us in our differences; here's to
our blood and tenderness, to sobbing
at the matinee, to tears and noses
wiped across our sleeves.

To dependent relationships—the pain they cause!
To the human mind ever-inventing
nuclear fission and the lobster bib—
to Beckett's sadness and the snow
on Issa's cheek, to our common
elements and to
the chicken, the stupid, enthusiastic
who fell beyond himself and loved
a pick-up truck—to the farmer,

asleep by now, who knows
just what he knows: that food
comes up out of the earth
and we go down into it,
that we are brief, and love,
whatever of, is love.

Apartment (2003)
—Erika Meitner

Hunting the classifieds for a rental, coffee
in front of me cold, this dark Hungarian pastry shop

is my only refuge, belonging to no one expect
the counter kid banging on the bathroom door, yelling

at the junkie inside: *I know what you're doing in there!*
I'm calling the police if there's blood on the walls again!

The couple sitting next to me—thin man
with glasses and a blue button-down, heavyset woman

in a stained undershirt—are drinking tea, playing poker
with a deck of tarot cards. Whose destiny

are they screwing with today? Everyone
is paired off, even this newspaper, reproducing

into endless sections. An article in the Metro Report:
a sneaker dredged up from the East River

might lead to a whole lost couple. The neighbors
hadn't seen them in weeks. The landlord was a suspect—

something to do with rent control. Cohabitation
was never a wise idea; not in this place

where apartments are treasures
found with chance and diligence

bribery and the occult. I was
your voodoo girlfriend, walk-up princess.

I am a wall. I can't open that way—
easily, like unlatching a suitcase.

My bags are packed; in was always your place.
Keep it. There were roaches climbing in the tub,

the exposed brick made it a prison, the stairs were endless,
and the neighbors—he sat on the couch all day,

she worked all night. He wouldn't do the dishes,
take the trash out. We would turn up the music, fuck,

anything to drown their yelling until finally we gave in,
put our ears to the floor. Listen:

the neighbors are still waiting
I can't split open like a bean.

Do you know how long their bodies
soaked in the river? There's no comparison.

Along the River of Palms (2014)
— Ravi Shankar
with Mong Lan

The discordance between thinking and though
is an illusion—all is a dance that leads you
from the past to the future and the present rolls forever
flat up/down
a seductive train of our own willpower.
Beside the plastic cow in the miniature railway set,
the tiny man in the peaked cap's facial expression
nearly changes ages nonetheless
the track looped as the sign for infinity.
Didn't we see that barn before?

Nope. We've never seen that barn
nor these fields nor these cows
which moo hopelessly echoing like mirrors
to other cows living in other dimensions
plastic and of the flesh and mooing blood
if it is mooing that we can call that lowing
ruminant mortality. Like the colosseum, the barn
a relic soon to be threshed by vines in/out
else bulldozed for strip malls to manifest,
new dishes for the feast of the hunter's moon

or the solstice moon of the moon that lows
and bellows the names of all lovers
that suffer and continue to exist
apart in a parallel world
where this world and the other is looped
a Mobius strip infinity
eating its own tail an ouroboros
digesting its own shadow while those relics—
that number scrawled in eyeliner on a napkin,
abalone and antler choker bought from Navajos,
the deck of fading Polaroids of the two of you
held together by a rubber band, shoved in the back

of the closet—decay slowly in half lives
like radioactive isotopes

yes   the two of you rubber-banding
even with the inevitable decay into something
else leading you to think you never existed
the two of you never existed
mere atoms with so much space in between
that you could walk through walls
wormholes into other futures
that never happened except here
the memory of stubble under the tongue
remembered view of an esplanade many stories
above face postage-stamped to the glass
made one and undone the two of you
mere rivulets along the river of palms

a river of penguins a stream of fierce wind
that makes everything undone
blowing the past away in one clean stroke
white on black and striped over the third eye
the future   empty and patient
filled with the moon on which we live
an alternate reality where all color is washed
away so that every emanation exists as pure
potential   a state of aboutness
in which time salts each body waddling
into and out of burrows in ecstatic display

time limed with salt
and each male body wails
for his counterpart
a rock under
water and she rises hearing him
responds to his grief-stricken song
with winged vibrations   a ritual dance
ancient as the sound at the center of stars
being born   brightening and dimming

in orbit and oscillation a burst here, a void there,
light seeking light, space the medium of time
until pinprick of awareness grows more glow

the glow of winged vibration glow of a face singed with song
what happens is mere dust
                                        dust to rise and dusk to finish
the napkin with a lipsticked kiss
is found in her pocket
her fingers twitch over the greasy red evidence
past crumbled into the future desire the arc of a shooting
star blotted in the napkin of the sky
a passageway to where the tongue loses itself
in guttural sound raw and radioactive
shuddered to keening contraction of starlight and dust
in perpetual dance.

I Want Everything (2016)

— Patricia Jabbeh Wesley

How do you negotiate something you cannot see?
But the woman on the phone is laying out in minute

details, the outcome of so many years of her marriage.
Gate 11, Detroit Airport, such an odd number,

where a woman takes out all the ammunitions of voice
with calm precision. As if this were only a board

for flattening out donut dough. This phone call
is so serious, all of us passengers seated at the gate

are invited to listen. This is a matter for divorce, all
the property, partitioned in small portions right here,

amidst the airport's new carpeting, so hard, it feels
like stepping on steel, and the feet of already weary

passengers becoming brittle and sore, and the years
that knew nothing about her impending divorce

are poised for accounting. "Listen to me," she declares,
as if you could see her now at her kitchen sink, her

dress splattered with cheese and oil and the years.
A woman, already old enough to be sixty or seventy

or just fifty-nine. They tell me a white girl ages
differently than us hard bone, slow wrinkling-skinned

black girls. Maybe she's only my age, how can I tell?
"Five hundred thousand dollars in hard cash," she says.

This woman is calm, her voice so still, it has become
a windless thing, as if she'd already killed this man

in her heart years ago. She may have soiled many
pillows many nights; She may have crashed many

wine glasses after the consolation of wine bottles,
the comfort, temporary, but potent enough to wipe

away years indiscriminately. Maybe she'd laid it all
out years ago, waiting for the boy to grow up, for

little Jessica to find herself. Maybe she'd swallowed
hard during many hard nights. Maybe she'd waited

and grew tired of waiting. "Five hundred thousand,
upfront, the lake front property, five thousand dollars

of alimony each month and the 401k, oh, I meant,"
she smiles, gazing out the window, eyes, cold, tearful.

Who is she married to, Bill Gates? I shake my head.
Outside the gate, our plane waits. In a few minutes,

it will navigate the clouds, parting blue sky from
white puffy balls, slashing up clouds so the plane

can exhale, so it's passengers can stay breathing.
But how do we negotiate what we cannot touch

or feel? "I want it all," she says into the kind ears
of a smart phone. Good thing, a phone is now smarter

than a husband, smarter than the woman herself
who holds it with cold, sweaty hands, in this long

distance show. "Listen to me," the stranger woman,
divorcing her husband from Detroit, declares.

Detroit, what a place on which to lay out the issues
long distance. "I want everything, everything,

except him, of course. It's been a long hell," she
sighs hard and dry. "We're boarding now. Please."

Some Writing Prompts for Meditative Poems

1. The hero's journey is a familiar literary trope. In "Fisher Street," Thylias Moss takes us on a journey down the street, but also in her thought process, and we arrive at a destination. In your meditative poem, take us on a journey.

2. One of the hallmarks of the meditative poem is how it examines the big questions in very specific ways. Patricia Jabbeh Wesley begins her poem with a question and then pursues an answer. Ry beginning a poem with a question that needs to be answered through the empirical experience brought to life in the writing of the poem.

3. People often say, "Things happen for a reason," but we all have experiences in which "the reason" for an event hasn't revealed itself to us. Write a poem that includes the narrative of

such an event and meditate on what possible lesson can be found in it through the engagement of associative thinking.

4. Go back to Joseph Fasano's "Heraclitean." What are some teachings/philosophies that are important to how you view the world? How do you struggle with them? How has the world borne out that way of thinking? Write a poem in which you allude to that way of thinking while simultaneously writing the world around us.

5. Alice Anderson presents us to a meditation on the word "conviction"; Hayan Charara wonders about "Thinking America." Think about a concept/abstraction that can be brought to life through narrative, image, and lyrical sensibilities. Try to define the term in a poem.

Chapter Eight: On the Dramatic Poem

You may have noticed that when we talk about the narrator of the poem, we refer to him or her as the speaker. Many people believe that the speaker of a poem is the poet, but more often than not, the poet has donned a mask. The mask may resemble the poet or may look radically different from him or her. The Latin poet Catullus, often let it be known that Catullus was speaking. In the *ghazal*, a Persian form dating back to the thirteenth century, it's common for the poet to name himself in the poem's closing couplet. In *The Inferno* by Dante, it's Dante being led through Hell by Virgil. In recent history, the confessional poets[1] have furthered a belief that the poet and the person speaking are one and the same. Many contemporary performance poets emphasize the realness of their poetic identities. I once said that the speaker in my poems has shared a lot of my own experiences, but he's also been through a lot of things I can only imagine. My job is to imagine them. Despite the prevalence of the lyric *I* who resembles the poet, it should be remembered that there is a long tradition of poems being spoken in the voices of others.

Consider the verse plays of Shakespeare: each of those poetic lines are spoken by different characters. Or consider the long passages of epic poetry, for instance in *The Iliad*, when Odysseus mourns the death of Achilles—this isn't the poet Homer speaking, but the hero Odysseus. The notion of a poet taking on another voice, is as old as poetry itself.

The dramatic poem (also known as the persona poem) harkens back to the age when plays were written in poetry. The dramatic poem is written in the voice of somebody else. The persona poem, on the other hand attempts to clarify that the speaker is *not* the poet but somebody else. Somebody clearly

---

[1] Confessional poetry started in the late 1950s in America, popularized by Robert Lowell, Sylvia Plath, Anne Sexton, and others who emphasized highly personal details about their lives. Confessional poets, however, did more than just tell their stories.

defined in the poem. T.S. Eliot's famous poem "The Love Song of J. Alfred Prufrock" is his attempt at telling his readers: this is not me, but this guy named Prufrock speaking. Many times, a writer creates and identifies a character to talk in the poem; other times, the speaker may embody the voice of a preexisting character and give us new insights into her or him.

Dramatic poems, then, are written in first person. They can be lyrics or narrative or meditations: different characters process the phenomena of this world in different ways, and we can use the tools we've learned so far to explore ways characters process the world differently than we do. The power of the dramatic poem comes as much from what we learn about the persona (and probably, also, about the self) as it does from how that persona identifies itself as different from the poet. If in a short story, character is revealed, and in the novel character is explored, then in the poem, character is transcended. When you write a persona poem you are attempting to transcend—to go beyond—what we already know about this character or this sort of person.

> In graduate school, a professor said "Once you find your voice, you're stuck with it." A poet's voice is the distinct way she has of presenting herself in a poem; it includes phrasing, word choice, experience, diction, craft sensibilities, etc. That said, there are ways to explore and broaden a poetic "voice" just as there are ways for musicians to expand theirs (they may cover songs in a completely different genre, try different instrumentations, or, like the great David Bowie, create personae (Ziggy Stardust, Alladin Sane, the Thin White Duke, who actually perform the songs through him)). One way we grow as poets is not becoming "stuck" with our voices, and we do that by exploring the boundaries of voice, and challenging ourselves to try on different points of view and the language choices that come with them.

Tim Seibles, a master of the persona poem, often takes on the voice of pop cultural icons (often in the form of characters from childhood television shows and cartoons), as he does in this sample poem. Look at how he provides new insight into the character to whom his poem gives voice. What does he do to surprise us with this character? How do we think of the character differently? How are the persona's concerns made universal?

Commercial Break: Road-Runner, Uneasy (1997)

If I didn't know better I'd say
the sun never moved ever,

that somebody just pasted it there
and said the hell with it,

but that's impossible.
After awhile you have to give up

those conspiracy theories.
I get the big picture. I mean,

how big can the picture be?
I actually think it's kind of funny—

that damn coyote always scheming,
always licking his skinny chops

and me, pure speed, the object of all
his hunger, the everything he needs—

talk about impossible, talk about
the grass is always greener...

I am the other side of the fence.

You've got to wonder, at least a little,
if this could be a set-up:

with all the running I do—
the desert, the canyons, the hillsides, the desert—

all this open road   has got to
lead somewhere   else. I mean,

that's what freedom's all about, right?
Ending up where you want to be.

I used to think it was funny— *Roadrunner*
the coyote's after you   Roadrunner...

Now I'm mainly tired. Not that
you'd ever know. I mean

I can still make the horizon
in two shakes of a snake's tongue,

but it never gets easier out here, alone
with Mr. Big Teeth and his ACME supplies:

leg muscle vitamins, tiger traps,
instant tornado seeds.

C'mon! I'm no tiger.
And who's making all this stuff?

I can't help being a little uneasy.
I do one of my tricks,

a rock-scorching, razor turn at 600 miles an hour,
and he falls off the cliff, the coyote—

he really falls: I see the small explosion,
his body slamming into dry dirt

so far down in the canyon
the river looks like a crayon doodle.

That has to hurt, right?
Five seconds later, he's just up the highway

hoisting a huge anvil
above a little, yellow dish of bird feed—

like I don't see what's goin' on. C'mon!

You know how sometimes, even though you're
very serious about the things you do,

it seems like, secretly, there's a
big joke being played,

and you're part of what
someone else is laughing at—only

you can't prove it, so you
keep sweating and believing in

your career, as if that
makes the difference, as if somehow

playing along   isn't really

playing along as long as you're
not sure what sort of fool

you're being turned into, especially
if you're giving it one-hundred percent.

So, when I see dynamite
tucked under the ACME road-runner cupcakes,

as long as I don't wonder why my safety
isn't coming first in this situation,

as long as I don't think me

and the coyote are actually

working for the same people,

as long as I eat and
get away   I'm not really stupid,

right?   I'm just fast.

The poem's title sets up the scene: we know who's talking and what the context is for the soliloquy. By taking the Road Runner out of the situation in which we normally expect him, Seibles already gives us something new. Bringing such freshness to the familiar is one of the most difficult things to do with a persona based on pre-existing characters. We must build on what we already know about the subject without ruining the character. Many persona poems fail by either not revealing anything new about the character or by having the reader say, "I don't believe this character would do that." Instead, the poem has to oscillate between the world of the character and the world of the poem.

This poem's use of lineation is very interesting. Seibles uses two line stanzas which move the poem along at a good clip. Perhaps they represent the Road Runner and Coyote. Surely, the Road Runner seems keenly aware that maybe he and the Coyote might be working for the same people. It's a cause of some consternation for him. Again, the Road Runner is given more depth by the poem: he normally seems happy-go-lucky. Fast and silent, sticking out his tongue and wiggling it before going "meep meep." The poem reverts to a few single line stanzas near the end in order to remind us of the Road Runner's loneliness while simultaneously suggesting he has shaken these thoughts from his head. Notice, though, how those last two lines are also the source of some doubt:

get away   I'm not really stupid

right? I'm just fast.

The poem is a meditation in the end. As mentioned before, persona poems can be written in any mode. Consider: how does the meditation seem like an unlikely mode for the Road Runner? What does choosing a meditation do for the poem?

Writing about a preexisting fictional character can illuminate something that transcends the fictional realm of the character's existence. We can do the same with historical and familial personalities. Such writing allows us to explore what we know about the people around us, or (perhaps more importantly and more powerful) write about people we knew little about in order to engage or appreciate their stories and consider our own relationship to them. Rita Dove, in her Pulitzer-prize winning collection *Thomas & Beulah* brings to life her segregation-era/ Depression-era grandparents by allowing them to tell their stories. More recently, Michele Battiste, in *Uprising*, captures the lives of grandparents living in Soviet-occupied Hungary in the 1950s. Let's consider one of those poems to see how she embodies the voice of her grandmother Jutka.

July 12, 1952: Waiting (2013)

On nights the girls sleep deeply, I risk
Western radio, ghosted voices
whispering their enchantments.

If they woke, Zsuzsi would keep
quiet, but Erika could slip, or worse
denounce me. A good little Pioneer,

on guard against any whiff of Western influence.
But better for us that she's a model Communist,
not spitting Jóska's anti-Party drivel. The radio

sustains my neighbors, rallying them to resist,
teasing with hints of assistance when the time
comes. The men listen for clues to know

how and when the revolution will begin,
as if the U.S. is itching to liberate

us. That nonsense is no comfort to me.

I tune it to the gypsy music, prohibited
under the regime, and remember
how Jóska danced with me, then

Erszi, then the girls, each clutching
a leg, Zsuzsi on one foot, Erika the other,
lifted by their father's steps.

The details of this lyric poem (and it is a lyric as it only captures this moment by the radio) are surely not from Battiste's life, so we're aware of the other voice, and the poem provides "information" for us to know the contextual narrative behind the lyric.

As with writing from the point of view of a fictional character, it is important to realize that when writing in the voice of a historical or familial personae, the goal is to bring them to life, and that requires imagination (to write beyond the stories we know) and personality, which means our job is to imbue them with a voice that is distinctly particular from our own as poets. It's not enough to write what is known already; rather those details should be a spring board for us into exploring what we don't know.

More liberating, and of singular use to those who are used to writing fiction, is that you can write a persona poem in the voice of someone you create. Edgar Lee Masters, in his famous *Spoon River Anthology*, creates an entire community populated with people who tell their stories. One of my first persona poems was in the voice of a toll collector. Remember: it has to be apparent in the poem who is talking and he or she must be defined as different from the poet. To have a toll collector talk about being out in the woods outside his house in a first person meditation wouldn't allow for anyone to know it wasn't me. Just writing a first person poem and then stapling on the title: "My Cousin Marty After His Senior Prom" isn't writing a persona poem. The idea here is to be a good fiction writer, to take on a voice, to find the insights that persona's story will lead to, and realize the character you choose and what he or she says will say a lot about you, no matter what.

Poet Diane Seuss spent some time working with oral history from small town Michigan, and created a cast of characters whose voices she brought to life. Here's a lyric poem in the voice of small town diner's proprietor.

what Marge would say if she'd lived to say it: (2015)

thatched roof like the one on Stack's garage and inside
six stools covered in split red plastic, five booths, a cement

floor (I'm being honest about its frailties) and an oil heater
the kids gathered around drinking their cocoa, no I didn't

offer marshmallows, no I did not make my own pies,
simple fare, chili, burgers, grilled cheese, coffee, real

cream, the men liked it here because it wasn't home
and they liked me because I wasn't their wife, my own

husband at the Uptown drinking his case of beer a day
with George Stack and Charlie, yes I was bony but I had

a nice smile and that place wasn't called Tom's or
Marge and Tom's it was Marge's, such as it was

Whether there was an actual Marge among these oral histories doesn't matter: the character is not in our collective public history, and therefore she functions as fictional. Like all lyric poems, this one captures a moment: one of small-town life, of acceptance and defiance, of identity. The poet's other choices, such as the lack of capitalization and the failure to adhere traditional grammar rules, enact this defiance and identity. The title lets us know that we are in someone else's voice and provides us with a sense of who this woman is, and since she hadn't lived to say it, further enacts Marge's overall attitude.

Whether lyric, meditative, or narrative, the dramatic poem creates another level of mediation on the events of the poem by removing the traditional lyric self from the poetry and instead positing another point of view.

Things to Think about When Reading Dramatic Poems

The persona poem gives the poet significant leeway in terms of the other poetic modes she employs. Think about whether this is a dramatic narrative, meditative, or lyric poem, and ask the same questions you would ask of those poems. But then, remember, the writer made a choice to compose this poem in the persona. That fact should lead to a few of its own questions.

1. What mode is this poem written in? How does the choice of poetic mode reflect on the persona speaking?
2. Is this a character we recognize? If so, what does the writer do to create a new perspective of him or her? Why/how is it important?
3. If this is a character we don't recognize, how do we recognize the persona? How does the poem introduce the persona and why do we think it's written in this voice?
4. Consider what (if anything) we know of the writer and her previous work. How does the choice of persona relate to her other poems? What does persona choice reveal about the poet?
5. What does the persona's perspective add to the nature of the content of the poem? What does it add?

Now look back at the sample poems above, and run through those questions.

A Collection of Dramatic/Persona Poems

The following collection of dramatic poems was assembled to show the range of possibilities the persona poem affords the writer. Think about the way the poem reveals insights into these characters, whether we know them or not.

Otis Clay Talks About His Parents[2] (2016)
— Linda Blaskey

Now, Mama was from the Delta.
A housewife. Loved to sing.
Lordy. Yes indeed.
But it was only the Gospel could set loose
the lark in her throat.

She put her children to that path
and it worked a while—
us clapping God's glory up to the rafters,
sweating under those heavy robes.

But see, Daddy was a card shark,
blew in from Chicago. His faith
bone cold, like dice clacked in his folded hand.
Sundays? Just another day.

The only thing a boy from that union
could do to save his self was sing the blues.
Truth is, no other way to go.

Doña Josefina Counsels Doña Concepción Before Entering Sears (1995)
— Maurice Kilwein Guevara

Conchita debemos to speak totalmente in English
cuando we go into Sears okay   Por qué
Porque didn't you hear lo que pasó   It say
on the eleven o'clock news anoche que two robbers
was caught in Sears and now this is the part
I'm not completely segura que I got everything
porque channel 2 tiene tú sabes that big fat guy
that's hard to understand porque his nose sit on his lip

---

[2]American Blues singer/guitarist born 1942, died 2016.

like a elefante pues the point es que the robbers the police
say
was two young men pretty big y one have a hairy face
and the other is calvo that's right he's baldy and okay
believe me qué barbaridad porque Hairy Face
and Mister Baldy goes right into the underwear department
takes all the money from the caja yeah uh-huh the cash
register
and ira Mister Baldy goes to this poor Italian woman that I
guess would be like us sixty o sixty-five who is in the section
of the back support brassieres and he makes her put a big bra
over her head para que she can't see nothing and kneel
like she's talking to God to save her poor life
and other things horrible pero the point como dije
es que there were two of them and both were speaking
Spanish
y por eso is a good thing Conchita so the people at Sears
don't confuse us with Hairy and Baldy that we speak English
only
okay ready
Oh what a nice day to be aquí en Sears Miss Conception

Waylon Smithers, Jr.[3] (2013)
— Tom C. Hunley

When I first worked for Mr. Burns, my skin
was black, but ever since then I've been yellow.
Hey, one day we'll all die and shed our sins.
Until then let's just get along and mellow.

Mr. Burns my skin has been yellow
since I first spit-shined your shoes.
Let's chill out, sir. Let's mellow.

---

[3] This poem is in a fixed form called the pantoum. For more on the pantoum, see appendix 4.

My yellow skin has got the blues.

Mr. Burns, I spit-shined your shoes.
Let's be jolly, sir. Let's be gay.
My yellow skin has got the blues.
Even Malibu Stacy used to say,

Let's be jolly, sir. Let's be gay.
That's one of your drones, from Sector 7G.
Even Malibu Stacy used to say
he'd do anything for his little girl, Maggie.

That's one of your drones , from Sector 7G.
His wife sketched you in the nude; his baby shot you.
He'd do anything for his little girl, Maggie.
He's the star of this show, not you.

Marge Simpson did the portrait; Maggie shot you.
Hey, one day we'll all die and shed our sins.
Homer Simpson's the star, Mr. Burns, not you,
but I'd give you everything, even my skin.

The Fisherman's Wife (2005)
— Mia Leonin

Bread: our curse and benediction, the ever present sail
fluttering between feast and famine.

Over my husband's woolen shoulder, I watch the grainy
masthead
crumble into a stew of lobster and sea bass.

I hold this thin crust like an intimate note,
a message I carry for someone else.

They say fishing teaches men patience,

but it's the village that must learn to wait.

They say *He* will multiply fishes
and divide the loaves into a living bread.

I hold mine like the flag of a nation
now many years erased.

The vespers smolder and we rub crumbs
between our fingers, waiting to sop up what remains:

capers and garlic, Galilee sloshing
in the bottom of an iron pot.

Further out, Peter and Paul sleep, joined by the same ear,
the Fisherman's curved hook, lowering.

When Nancy Drew the Line (2001)
— Amy MacLennan

Some people think I've got it all.
Family money, perfect boyfriend
and quite the local reputation.
Just last week the headlines read,
"Girl Sleuth Foils Jewel Heist."
But I'm sick of hunting for clues in clocks,
sketching footprints and faces,
getting thrown in secret rooms
always bound and gagged.
And to be honest, Ned is a real bore.
I'd trade it all in,
the convertible, tailored clothes,
even the titian hair
(and it's red goddamn it)
for something bad.
I want to move out, get a job
modeling bathing suits

or designing tattoos.
Leave River Heights behind,
hitchhike to a real city
and drink peach daiquiris
in a downtown bar.
I've done the right thing my whole life.
Kept my father's house,
solved every case,
never broke the rules.
It's not easy being this good.

Mrs. Kessler (1916)

— Edgar Lee Masters

Mr. Kessler, you know, was in the army,
And he drew six dollars a month as a pension,
And stood on the corner talking politics,
Or sat at home reading Grant's Memoirs;
And I supported the family by washing,
Learning the secrets of all the people
From their curtains, counterpanes, shirts and skirts.
For things that are new grow old at length,
They're replaced with better or none at all:
People are prospering or falling back.
And rents and patches widen with time;
No thread or needle can pace decay,
And there are stains that baffle soap,
And there are colors that run in spite of you,
Blamed though you are for spoiling a dress.
Handkerchiefs, napery, have their secrets
The laundress, Life, knows all about it.
And I, who went to all the funerals
Held in Spoon River, swear I never
Saw a dead face without thinking it looked
Like something washed and ironed.

Medusa Cuts Her Hair (1998)
—Jean Monahan

Something in the curl wants out.

*

You think you know something about love,
have a clear idea of your own value.
Then your friends stop speaking
when you enter a room, turn a cold eye
on your antics, your pleas, your parting curse.

*

Lately, I've let myself go.
Strange thoughts spring from my scalp.
They have a life of their own.

I think about striking out, striking back.
I think about curling into a knot,
and never encircling another again.

*

What is it I keep hearing,
in waking and in sleep?
Little voices, secrets, fears.
Every wish I ever had, every hurtful
word I've said.
They do not leave, but hiss in the head,
weaving together until they sprout anew.
There are lies caught in my locks;
memories of happiness, too.

*

He said he was a hairdresser,
would trim my tresses
by looking into a mirror.
I agreed to keep my eyes lowered.
Think of it; the snip of scissors,
a strange man's fingers,
oil of aloe, henna, citrus.
Nervous, his limbs jiggled;
I fell in love with his legs
as he circled my chair.

*

Where is the man who cut my hair?
People tease me, say I've lost my head.
Now, the world softens under my stare.

My Father Talks of 1946 (2007)
—Christine Rhein

Expulsion is the method which, in so far as we have been able to see, will be the most satisfactory and lasting. There will be no mixture of populations to cause endless trouble . . .

> WINSTON CHURCHILL, 1944, after Stalin negotiated the expulsion of 15 million Germans from their ancestral homelands in East and West Prussia, Silesia, Pomerania, and the Sudetenland

The Poles loaded us into the same cattle cars
the Nazis had sent the other way.
They searched our sacks to make sure
there was nothing left worth stealing.
It was August 5th. A bit of bread
for what became a three-day ride.

Flüchtling—the word for refugee—
means one who flees, as if we had a choice,
or as if, after fifteen months of occupation,
soldiers taking over our house,
we weren't relieved to go.

Two million German civilians died
in the expulsion. Starvation, exposure,
torture, murder. You never hear of it.

Churchill kept his mouth shut.
And how could Germans talk about atrocity?

I was fifteen, suddenly a *Flüchtling*
in my own country, in a town where no one
understood our dialect, knew my surname.

Imagine it, if Texas were given to Mexico,
if the government delivered an El Paso mother
and four children to your door, ordered you
to give them a bedroom, share your empty pantry.

All I thought about was food.

Mother sent my sister and me out walking to the farms.
If they won't give you any potatoes, ask for only two.

The farm women scowled: *What will you do*
with only two? Oh here, take them!
When we had too many, we hid them in a ditch,
carried a few to show that others had given.

My aunt, who ended up in East Germany
with the other half of our village, sent me
my cousin's winter jacket. He had fallen
in Russia just before the war ended.

I had no shoes. Three times a week

Mother made me walk the hour
to the ration office. *Don't put anything*
on your feet or they'll never give you shoes.

Believe me, by November, it was cold.
I looked for grass to walk on
and dreaded the tile floor of the office,
the way adults tried to cut in front of me
because I wanted to stand on the doorway mat.

Don't think people didn't look out for themselves.

One day, the woman behind the window
whispered, *It's here*, snuck me out the back door
as she handed me the little certificate.

In the store, I picked out work shoes.
After years of *Learn! Learn!*
my parents no longer talked of school.

Bricklaying seemed like a good idea
in a land of rubble.

Some Writing Prompts for Dramatic Poems

1. Consider a family member you know little about but whose story or some anecdote about him or her intrigues you. Using the narrative that you know, let him or her speak about the relevance of this moment to him or her. Or, better yet, put them in an entirely different situation (one in direct opposition to the story you may know) and allow them to reflect on that.

2. Many personas come with a "form" for what they say; for instance, Captain Kirk has the captain's logs; Dr. Jeckyll has lab notes; Julia Child comes with recipes. Using that form as a starting point for working with content, write a persona poem

that uses the character's "formal vessel" as a means of controlling the poem.

3. Change is the crux of personal evolution. Look at Jean Monahan's "Medusa Cuts Her Hair." Now consider something a character is famous for and have him or her alter that one thing. For instance, "Frodo Baggins Pawns the Ring of Power" or "Harry Potter Gets Contact Lenses." Remember, the implicit question that gives such scenarios power is why does this person make this dramatic change.

4. Write a poem in the voice of someone who never got to tell his or her own story that you know well. Remember to make it clear why this story is important and who this person is as a full-fledged character.

5. Find a story in the News of the Weird, *The Guinness Book of World Records*, or *The Weekly World News* and write in the voice of one of these people who have done things obsessively (clapped her hands for 79 hours, 33 minutes straight) or have done something bizarre (taxidermied animal thief), or seen something bizarre (Girl Scout who Sold Cookies to UFO Tells her Story).

Chapter Nine: On the Post-lyric/Fractal Poem

Poetry has often been an experimental art form, and, as it became less an oral art, many of those experiments have been played out in how the poem "uses" the page. In the early seventeenth century, George Herbert's "Easter Wings" was conceived so that the stanzas resembled pairs of angel wings. Throughout the Modernist era, we see poets exploring how indentations and line lengths can have an effect on the presentation of the poem, and in the later twentieth century, concrete poetry, in which poems were written so that the text on the page resembled an object was not unusual. Other experimentations, such as L-A-N-G-U-A-G-E poetry, focused on the limitation of words as signifiers and explored the potential for a poetry based primarily on syllabic sounds.

The post-modern era with its focus on multiple voices, its connection to the post-atomic age (with its multiple dimension theories), has developed its own lyric sensibility. As with the traditional lyric, its focus is the moment, but it explodes the moment into its pieces. If the lyric poem is an atom; the post-lyric looks at the subatomic particles that compose an atom. Or to use the term *fractal* (as some, particularly poet Alice Fulton, call it), which is commonly defined as "a geometrical or physical structure having an irregular or fragmented shape"; the mathematician Benoit Mandelbrot coined the term, which he took from the Latin fractus, meaning an irregular surface like that of a broken stone. In math, fractals are a way to understand chaos. By association, the fractal poem engages the very chaos it tries to order. Fulton notes that her "prospectus for post modern fractal poetry suggested that digression, interruption, fragmentation, and lack of continuity be regarded as formal functions rather than lapses into formlessness" (Thumbscrew 12).

The post-lyric then is often personal, and it endeavors to express the experience of the moment; but rather than order the chaos, it tries to say chaos *is* the lyric experience and embraces it as such. Rather than trying to be a compass that settles on true north, such poems accept disorientation. A fractal poem might include multiple voices (in the form of other people talking, found material, etc.), memory, associative thought, and other "random" elements to show the lyric event in all its jagged (fractured) glory. It will also avoid adhering to the orderliness of the left margin.

Post-lyric poems then use elements of lyricism, but their focus is to not accept but to enact complexity. It says experience isn't smooth and clean, so the poem shouldn't be clean either. Formally, such poems may have multiple sections, indentations, footnotes, an excessive use of "white space," and prose passages. It may begin with punctuation (often a dash or a colon) or a conjunction, so it seems as if we enter mid-thought. The fractal poem sees the page as a fluid place where the poem's pieces can be placed to allow the reader to participate in the emotional, linguistic, intellectual, and spiritual fragmentation expressed. Despite this chaos, there remains (or there should remain) a logic to this use of fracture, a kind of *geometry* of poetics as it were, beneath the chaos.

> White space is the area on the page devoid of text. Some poems have lines that are so long they "wrap around" and are indented from the left margin to show that they are part of the line above. Poet Charles Wright uses a line he calls the "low rider" which *drops* part of the way across the page so our eye continues to the right getting the visual effect of a line break but the rhythmic effect of a regular line. Poets can use indentations of other sorts to make the eyes dart around the page, to "shape" the poem, or to allow for multiple voices to appear. Remember, everything we do with the page changes the reader's expectations and how she approaches the poem, and there ought to be a rationale as to why you're manipulating the page in this way.

Poet Mary Ann Samyn has worked with lyric and fractured lyric poems for much of her writing career. Here's one of her more fractal poems that fuses found text with lyric experience, meditative moments, humorous tonal shifts (look at how she uses the parenthetical), and other voices.

A Career Guide for Girls

— Then the question behind the other question

"Are you service
oriented?"

(Are you a hot or cold beverage?)

In other words, here are your choices:
teacher nurse stewardess,
some helping
profession, some *oh you*

Poor thing you—

Is there anything I can—

Sir—?

NoNoNo
This is not your big, brave famous—,
is it?

Oh, come on now.

She left suddenly, is what they'll say
if you don't tell.

She flinched *south.*

As though you weren't oriented
properly.

As though you couldn't manage
a compound

you.

For example: home + maker
or house + wife

such nice words!

As though the oven loves you. (The red coil: *hiss hiss*)

As though the early American wallpaper
isn't too too
busy–

Housewife means

married/small
woman/container
who/sewing
supervises/affairs
equipment/household

—But you knew that, didn't you?

Felt it like a sick headache,
in bed, all day, wishing
for a solid noun, a better verb.

> Some poems use what is called "found text," material from other works that is re-purposed for the poem. Found text is often italicized to allow the reader to know these words are not the poet's or speaker's.

As you can see, the poem attempts to come to terms with a moment of understanding what it means to be a woman. By engaging found material (from a book from the fifties titled *A Career Guide for Girls*), the poem balances various tones (including the speaker's inner sarcastic voice) and resolves the chaos in open-ended fashion.

The poem begins with a dash, to let us know we are entering mid-thought. To put it another way, we enter a broken thing, and we are not privy to the entire discussion (or even the details if it). Fracture, therefore, is a part of the poetic experience on a grammatical level as well as a formal level.

The poem further uses the page in such a way that our eyes remain "uncertain" of where to go next, highlighting the "rough surface" of experience. As with much of what happens, the poem comes at us from different directions, and it delivers that to us formally as well as tonally.

So what are the hallmarks of the post-lyric/fractal poem?

- They function as almost meta-lyric poems, working as lyric poems do, but providing a concurrent alternative moments, commentary, and reflection.
- They use the page in a fragmented way.
- They bring in multiple voices/tones/texts into the mix, including, but not limited to, found texts.
- They use punctuation as a way of breaking apart the sentence, moving us syntactically as well as formally, etc.
- They work associatively.

Things to Consider When Reading Post-lyric/Fractal Poems

The post-lyric poem is about fracture, about the multiplicity of experience. It suggests that what happens to us doesn't happen in a vacuum, but rather it rubs up against schema—both personal and cultural—that helps us contextualize and understand the event. Rather than smooth over such schema, the post-lyric poem attempts to present the chaos, thereby enacting the multiplicity of its subject.

Here are some things to ask as we read fractals. These are just meant to guide you when thinking about post-lyric poems you might encounter.

1. What is the "lyric moment" of the poem? How do the various aspects of the poem present the experience? How are we to

engage the tiles of the poem to make them make a picture that makes sense?

2. What are the various tones of the poem? Are their found texts or other voices in the poem? How do they ask us to engage them? How do they shine (different) lights on the experience?
3. What is the structure of the poem–line and stanza? How does the poem use the page differently and to what effect? How do such movements on the page teach us to read the poem? How does the page make meaning?
4. What are the keys to the poem? Images? Tones? How do we know this?

So let's put this sort of basic reading into practice. Here's a poem by Carl Phillips, another lyric poet whose work sometimes engages fracture.

Since You Ask (2012)

Through the air, over water,
five crows are taking down a falcon—

it's like a dream:

dream-falcon
deposition
mercy-falcon

the wings folding and unfolding like
any childhood looked at

then looked away from, across it

warriors spurring on forever their still half-wild horses,
rivers to ford, still,
slaughter ahead—bullet, arrow—horses

included, *if you must,*
then swiftly, despite whatever in a horse might count

as innocence, X, but glittering, let it

split the fair steed's forehead clean in two.

1. The poem's title sets us up in mid-thought: something has been asked and now here's the answer. The question is left unstated, so we have to determine/decipher what was asked by the context of the poem. We can almost imagine this to be the answer to "How are you feeling?" as to "What are you looking at?" Surely, the poem engages an existential sensibility that suggests more the former question than the latter, but without such clarity, the jagged edge of this poem's fractal nature reveals itself from jump.
2. Obviously we have a moment of dream tone in the poem early on—those indented moments that enact bird flight but that include the odd word, "deposition" which may be the key word to the poem. Then we get a bit of external text/voice: "*if you must,/then swiftly,*" which we can't know where it comes from, but which is important. If we accept the slaughter as metaphoric (which is safe to assume), then whatever hurt or grief is being remembered the speaker wants to happen quickly (better to have it happen fast than to linger). The X—a moment of mathematics, the unknown—is another bit of found language. The whole poem asks us, in some way, to solve for X.
3. This poem doesn't use much in the way of white space, with the exception of the dream moment early in the poem, and the last line. The dream falcons get to fly, but they also allow for the word "deposition" to appear as a line unto itself, outlying on the right margin. (Note how there are five crows and there are five words in the flying stanza.) This emphasizes the import. Is this a dream deposition or a real one? And what's the context for it? A divorce perhaps (this is me reading into the poem and how it moves to childhood)? This would set us up both for the "slaughter" later on, and for the answering of the question. The last line is interesting because the indentation is a splitting, the poem enacts the

meaning of the last clause by breaking the sentence both across two stanzas but then cleaving the margin.

4. The poem is about feeling hunted. The falcon is hunted by crows but we think, normally, of falcons being the hunters. It is a "mercy-falcon," which creates all sorts of questions about the situation. Someone who is usually the hunter is the aggrieved. This leads to childhood—the warriors on horseback (Native Americans based on the arrows), and "still/slaughter ahead" (the warriors go to *be* slaughtered). The line break on "still," holds the lyric moment. The poem, ultimately, is about the loss of innocence, that thing, that unknown/unknowable X, that splits the horse's forehead in two, that leads us into adulthood's complicated thinking.

A Collection of Fractal Poems

The fractal poem is a post-modern poem, so the samples are more recent. Look at the variety of ways fragmentation, "inter-dimensionality," and multiple perspectives, and remember to consider the questions above.

Fragments from Childhood (2014)
— Abdul Ali

Fragment from Childhood #8

fold-up cot
    radiator misting, a high soprano

                                                            my nose bleeds
midnight
    marauders squeak in the trash

                                                            Fragment from
Childhood #23

                                                            There's a pigeon
on the fire escape

I want to follow
the pigeon to the edge.

Double Dare me?

I'll fly.

Fragment from Childhood #36

A loud gasp from behind my mother's door
I entered her room with a screwdriver and begin
stabbing air
Two voices shriek, wait!—

Fragment
from Childhood #43

An old-fashion Coca-Cola bottle cap nicks my left eye
A steady red flow tints my vision.

Semantics (2006)
— Erica Dawson

Right now I much prefer
Darkie in place of African-
American—the melanin
More obvious. As per
Political Correct-
Ness, wait, I'll reconsider Black:
Reflecting little light, a lack
Of predominant hue—effect
Very dark.

*

This black, Mom said,
Was born when an up-north matriarch
Got hitched back in the day, went dark

In Texas. Brillo head
Met roller hair, a lean
And knobby knee wearing a layer
Of darker skin. Our jaws curve square
And round, some aubergine
("Blue black"), some fair. Some who?
Darkies. Remember? I'm in question.
So when a man asked (with suggestion?),

*

"You got Indian in you?"

*

I told him Black and yes,
Characterized by cheerless sullenness.
No light, pictured in an evening dress,
I smile, incandesce,
And flash. My teeth are white.
The rest is shadow.

*

Perceptions of
Black appear to depend (above)
On the contrast with bright
And colored stimuli.
Black: zero stimulation to
The retina.

*

A vision too
Invisible? I try
To block the light, eyes closed,
But I'm at perihelion.
Even the Tiffany lamp's a sun
And I am too exposed.

*

Some days I just see red.

*

Outside, twisting like ivy stems,
My black is brown as problems
And the empty flowerbed

Collecting rain. Is sheen
More relevant, more true, than hue?
And do I shine? This jigaboo
Moves here in shades of green.

A Letter from Iceland (1998)
— Cynthia Hogue

Furious the roses where he once drew blood.
Cutting oneself, opening up feels new
(And new my soul).

Still, one reasons,
the remarkable
gets by us, not sleight of hand
but subtle. We flit about,
hummingbirds,
our hearts
reft with nebulous longing.

Who is this person?
Where did he come from?

How do we know
when not to drop to

ground level,
nearer the new
blossoms, bury
our faces in them?

He writes of new love
(I know you told me not to!).
We have no memory or desire,
simply read the letter.

It is no longer our life.
We do not bleed.

Spacetime (1995)
— Miroslav Holub *Trans. by David Young and Dana Hábová*

When I grow up and you get small
then—

(In Kaluza's theory the fifth dimension
is represented as a circle
associated with every point
in spacetime)

—Then when I die I'll never be alive again.
Never.
Never never?
Never never.
Yes, but never never never?
No ... not never never never,
Just never never.

So we made
a small family contribution
to the quantum problem of eleven-dimensional
supergravity

Divided Interior[1] (2013)
— Ailish Hopper

After the Rising, looting. The British prop a wounded rebel,
just so they can shoot him.
Yeats: *too long a sacrifice can make a stone of the heart.* In the
city named Unvisited.

When Revere called out, *One if by— two if by sea*, he meant
Begin.
All signals, a way to touch—*Over all of Spain, the sky is clear—*
what must appear unvisited.

Because they're hard to see, I listen for the doors' close. In
the questions— *So*
and micro-second's pause, to my mother's answer, *Oh—*,
when we become unvisited.

Slow-dances in our discotheque: twilit shed, BBC. With a
Protestant boy, I *let him feel*,
body listening. Then he whispers, *American, not Catholic?* and
gets unvisited.

Ailish, the codes—*The princess wears red shoes*—seem
innocuous as children's rhymes. But
symbols seep—*The Catholic one is by the sea*—deep into muscle,
bone. What cell is not unvisited?

---

[1] Besides being an example of fractal poetics with its multiple voices, this poem is also a ghazal. For more on this form, see appendix 4.

Dorothy Arzner Looks in the Lens of her Camera and Sees Caroline Herschel's Comets Falling through Adrienne Rich's Eyes[2]

— Patrick Lawler

Inside the camera everything looks squished.

Devoured by the   glass lens,   I'm tiny.

I am sitting in an empty theater
waiting for a movie to come on.
My waiting   is the movie.

It's just like Andy Warhol—except it's tedious.

I'm watching previews of my dreams
and feel my body   fill with sight.

When my clothes
catch fire,
I take that
as a sign.

I am making a movie of this woman's mouth.
    She is a book
of light   I can never close.

And then the director asks:
Who do you think you are?

Someone is playing John Wayne and he is mad.
Someone is playing Marilyn Monroe and she is sad.

---

[2] Dorothy Arnzer was a silent-era movie director. Caroline Herschel was a nineteenth century astronomer who discovered several comets. Adrienne Rich was a twentieth century feminist poet.

Etc. Etc.

I am sitting in front of an empty silver window.
The only thing I have left is this fear of asphyxiation.

I hear:
                    Cut.
                      Cut.

And I know exactly what it means.

I take up again the issue of   the   real
and enter a poem by Adrienne Rich.

It gets scary at this point.

I have melted   into the camera.
Hollywood is killing my identity, but I feel happier this way.

Here the movie changes direction.

The telescope swallows.

Motorcycles like hornets in a coffee can.
Crash scenes. Bullets.   Flying.

The movie changes direction.   Everything is soft.
            In the last scene, I am living with a woman's mouth.
The aquarium where my heart grows.

Cut.

Cut.
Cut.
I look at the world around me and know exactly what it means.

A Study of Bird Song (2011)

—Sandy Pool

with text incorporated from *A Study of Bird Song*, published 1963

Bird Utterance as Language

> To recognize a rival by its song.
> Graceful as a neck, makeshift
> plumage. Do not tell me about love,
> augmented sound. It's syntax
> I want, gesture, the old territorial
> songs.

Sub-song

Belligerent threat. One cock

crowing. No response.

Acoustic Communication and the organs involved

> To sing, whole-heartedly and without regret. If
> evolution has followed this path we may suppose
> that song, like visual display, is the product of
> conflicting impulses. Song and display

may be

regarded

as resultants

of the

transference of conflict

from the environment to within.

Any

amateur birder

can note the difference,

the predatory

pitch.

(iv) Vocal Mimicry

There are many imitations. To deny
this would be denying the existence
of God, thin brush of wind. Your
terrible silhouette retains its outward
notions, honest as a killdeer, pleading.

Apparently, birds may learn mimicries not only
in a state of emotional rapport but in the contrary
emotional condition.

Art. Love. Geology. (1995)
— Bin Ramke

Ist es schön, in der Sonne zu gehn —Trakl

Here is a little book of instructions. It says care
must be taken. For instance, a form of health as a
version of vanity (as when a poor stonecutter set up
shop to live off the vanity of travelers, pioneers
who stopped to scratch names and dates in inviting surfaces
but granite is hard on the amateur so a graffitist

*

an American artist against the rapacious
rock body of the earth did cover the good body with
American names, this natural poetry which must be
written carelessly before the one wall, after the other.
The view was magnificent, and the air smelled of future)
                vanity in this world, my Dear, your hair the color,
this kind of poetry, this world tells itself stories,
O famous your green shoes your fabulous wishes your
hair the color of tea and your green shoes aren't you
      something.
It says here you must listen to your own history, it says
you must take care, and it says here you must pronounce
your name, your own name here ____________________.

*

The man did believe in the monochrome
possibilities, the way the camera would focus
such a narrow range of color thus the *sharpness*
of the old photographs, the clarity of vision
of the American West before the development
of panchromatic films. And the movies, the cow-
boys and Indians blazing black and white.

*

"At the edge of the forest/Stillness encounters
a dark deer"—the ways she said it, my friend
said it of Trakl, his poem. *Geitsliche Dämmerung*
and it is snowing now and cold. When I knew her
we were young and the age of earth indeterminate.
Forests had edges. Deer were a species of Indian.

*

Here is the world come to comfort me. Here
is a child come to follow me home.

*

The traveling salesman said to the farmer's daughter:
we are in the world together and there is no place
to sleep, so let's join hands and sing of the glory
and honor of the forest and its deer which watch us;
see their eyes reflect the light, see them wait for us.

*

Und rings ergläntzen Hügel und Wald.

*

And surrounding us, you and I, love,
something like the night—at least it is dark,
at least it is silent. It seems to move
only when we do not look at it. It seems
to be the world, but who knows, and we,
do we really care more for each other
than the world, can the songs be right?

*

Surrounding shimmering in ultraviolet
the darkness to our eyes not our own, but we
have gauges to measure the shimmer.
The insects see in light not ours
the insects see flowers in violets so deep
its darkness shimmers in the corners of
my eye as if I made it up.

*

If hills emerge too slowly to see, still, evidence
remains—it's what geology says, that this earth
moves beneath each lover, slow and impossible
but there you have it, the hills rise around us
when we are not looking and one day an alp.
taps you on the shoulder as you kiss
and you mind wasn't on the time; it is late.

*

This is the forest, here, we live here. Arboreal
safety. Who cares for evolution. Here, let me
love you then we'll fall from the trees like
fruit, the sound it makes, the forest surrounds
our racial despair. Oh how we hate to be human.

Some Writing Prompts for Fractal Poems

1. Patrick Lawler's poem gets some of its energy from the quality fo the mash-up: he takes several things that don't go together and puts his knowledge of them to create a mosaic. Furthermore, because this is also a dramatic poem in the voice of early Hollywood director Dorothy Arzner, more fracture is instilled into the poem. Consider taking information you know about two or three different figures and re-mix them together.

2. Find a book of arcane knowledge, or a book from 75 years ago, or a magazine article that is designed to teach you something. Using this found text, write a poem that engages the material, the reason why the speaker is thinking about the material, and a sense of "marginalia"—side bar commentary—that makes it apparent why the speaker finds this text "important."

3. Think back to an important conversation, preferably one from several years ago. What was the context of the conversation? Why is it one you remember today. Piece together snippets of the conversation (particularly the other person's words), the context for the conversation, and why this conversation is still relevant to form a poem that engages the fractured sense of experience.

4. The art of montage is the way of creating a narrative with only glimpses of images unconnected by any narrative thread. Using only lyric fragments, including other voices and images and found text (perhaps television dialogue or song lyrics), create a montage poem.

Afterthoughts

Chapter Ten: No Ideas but in Things

We've gotten through the primary modes of poetry. We've spoken about the importance of the image. The Modernists, who developed Imagism, had a saying, *Make it new*, which implores poets to not settle for tired metaphors, to avoid cliché, and to consider the energy for both the reader and writer in developing new associative leaps through the image.

For years poets have focused on objects and studied them. Our relationship to the things of this world are important, whether we are speaking in terms of ownership (consider how possessive we are, even in love we talk about *my* girlfriend or *my* husband), but also in terms of how we experience the world around us. One person's beautiful walk in the woods is another person's role as mosquito buffet. As poets, we can define the world of things through the ode and the descriptive poem.

The traditional ode had the poet celebrate an object (consider Keats's "Ode on a Grecian Urn," "Ode to a Nightingale," "Ode to Autumn"); often such poems explored as much the poet's thoughts on the item in question as they did the object themselves. Although many of the classical odes have a fixed formal element, most contemporary odes have shed this element. In their terrific anthology *Breathe: 101 Contemporary Odes*, Ryan VanCleave and Chad Prevost define odes as the great Roman poet Horace would: "meditative lyrics on a variety of themes" (8). The ode is a way to delve into the imaginative and philosophic possibilities of a particular subject. In the contemporary American aesthetic, the ode functions not in the trappings of versification but in the process that draws out thought. The goal of the ode is to bring to life a meditative poem with all the hallmarks of such, based on rhapsodizing or ruminating on a particular object.

Consider this opening of Shelley's "Ode to the West Wind," a Romantic-era poem composed in five sections:

O wild West Wind, thou breath of Autumn's being,
Thou, from whose unseen presence the leaves dead
Are driven, like ghosts from an enchanter fleeing,

Yellow, and black, and pale, and hectic red,
Pestilence-stricken multitudes: O thou,
Who chariotest to their dark wintry bed

The wingèd seeds, where they lie cold and low,
Each like a corpse within its grave, until
Thine azure sister of the Spring shall blow

Her clarion o'er the dreaming earth, and fill
(Driving sweet buds like flocks to feed in air)
With living hues and odours plain and hill:

Wild Spirit, which art moving everywhere;
Destroyer and Preserver; hear, O hear!

Written in terza rima, this poem brings in myth and fancy, creates comparison between Autumn and Spring, and begins to contemplate on the nature of the wind itself. The ode then, might be thought of as a type of meditative poem that focuses its attention on a particular thing—an animal, a mood, and object. Shelley addresses the wind, so as to implicitly personify the wind: if we can address it, it can understand what's being said. As with all meditations, the person doing the meditating is equally important, and the goal is to allow the reader to consider this object as well. Anything can be the focus of the ode's meditation.

When thinking about the ode as a reader, it's a good idea to consider the questions we should ask about any meditative poem (see page 95). After all, it's the meditative quality of the ode that makes it a powerful celebration of the subject.

Aside from the ode, another way we examine the world around us is in the metaphoric remaking of it. One might argue that "seen one pigeon, you've seen them all," and that might seem true. The artist, however, needs to constantly see the world with a kind of awe, a kind of possibility, and one way to do that, then, is to constantly re-imagine it, to literally put it in an image again. Metaphor, then, becomes a way to reestablish the phenomena of the world. As D.G. James puts it, "[w]hen ... the poet uses metaphor, he abandons the merely informative method; yet, at the same time, he suggests the inner quality of the objects" (95).

It helps to remember that the ancient Talmudic rabbis used to say that there was a spark of god in every element of creation. Plato suggested that for everything that is there is an ideal version of it that we all have in our heads. The descriptive poem attempts to re-describe something ordinary to find what's extraordinary about it. Taking a page from haiku masters, Imagist poets focused their attention on re-envisioning the world around them. These poets didn't need to think about the object, so much as to reinvent it, to find in the item a metaphoric epiphany. Such poems present a kind of lyric under-standing in which the nature of the item in question is transcended through the act of the poem.

> Many poets say that poems aren't about subject matter; rather, they're about the way we handle subject matter, the way we think about it. The ode and the descriptive poem are, however, about both subject matter *and* how we handle it. Many poets have written poems that focus just on animals, for instance, creating what is called a bestiary, a collection of poems that ask us to reconsider ordinary animals. Whatever our subject matter, though, the success of the poem is grounded in how we get the reader to look at the subject in new ways.

T.S. Eliot, one of the most famous English-language poets, discussed the notion of the objective correlative—basically, an object (image) that correlates to an abstraction as such to define it for us in new ways. Many of these short descriptive poems are pure uses of the correlating object.

It's good when thinking about writing the short descriptive poem to keep in mind this definition of Imagism, which is ascribed to both Ezra Pound and F.S. Flint:

1. Direct treatment of the "thing," whether subjective or objective.
2. To use absolutely no word that does not contribute to the presentation.
3. As regarding rhythm: to compose in sequence of the musical phrase, not in sequence of the metronome.

Thus, a descriptive poem is a focused lyric that helps us re-envision a particular item, and by doing so questions the very nature of perception, as in this poem by the imagist Amy Lowell.

Sunshine (1915)

The pool is edged with the blade-like leaves of irises.
If I throw a stone into the placid water,
It suddenly stiffens
Into rings and rings
Of sharp gold wire.

Notice how Lowell sets us up for sunshine, but then holds off presenting it. We get the scene (the pool, the irises), but the sunlight isn't mentioned outside of the title; it can only be presented when it reveals itself. In this poem the speaker is the bringer of transformation: only by throwing the stone does the sunlight appear in ripples the rock makes, and the pool is changed into something man-made. We might think, then, that the poem is a metaphor for the art of poetry making: by writing poems we transform the world around us.

Such poems remind us that the world has many ways to see it, and by transcending the object's normal experience, we create lyricism. Thus the goal is to "re-imagine" the ordinary—that's true creative writing.

As with the ode, to consider the descriptive poem when we read it, it might be best to look again at the questions we ask of more traditional lyrics.

Lastly, let's remember it's not just the things of the world that poets can re-imagine through the ode and the descriptive poem. Many poets have written about abstractions in an attempt to define them (Keats famously wrote an "Ode on Melancholy), in an attempt to create imagistic metaphors for the abstraction. Another way to consider these poems is to write about places, to make us re-see a particular location. Look again at Evelyn Lau's "Las Vegas" (page 61), and see how the observational lyric becomes a way of recreating that city.

Landscape, of course, is not an unusual subject matter for poets; it's often been said that the external landscape mirrors the internal, and most writers have a complicated sense of place. Federico Garcia Lorca wrote his famous *Poet in New York* as a way of giving fresh eyes to Manhattan, particularly those of an outsider. Richard Hugo in his book *The Triggering Town* talks about his and other poets' relationship to cities as jumping off places for poetry.

Steven Leyva does this in his poem, "Baltimore," which gives us a different perspective of that city than *The Wire,* the national news, or John Waters movies. Instead, we get an insider's perspective of the streets transformed by weather.

Baltimore (2013)

It's snowing again. 20 inches
dumped down the throat
of the city, the cobble

streets between Bond and Broadway are leveled.
The awful rectitude of ice, hewn in salt-laced
stoops, shames the old and young. Snow flattens

car hoods and fills a rowhome shell. In the bald
backyard behind Wilkens Ave. A layer of broken
glass and dismembered toys holds up the snow.

The alley erased isn't mourned. A block east
Henderson's toboggan, its brim half folded
surrenders to a stone packed in a snow ball.

Snow piles in parks, and when Bobcats begin
shoveling again—1st attempt a small one flipped
and crushed a man—parks bloat like an orphan stuffed

with gruel. Snow remains white less than a day. Tires grind in
black, hand shovels raise the dead asphalt, dogs mark and
mock
weak sun. Whole neighborhoods fill prescriptions at the
liquor

store. A fight breaks out over a dug parking spot, and after
a couple
of punches, someone breaks a gin bottle. Peace. Another
bustle
in clouds drops a foot more. The drifting banks cancel the 1st
floor

over an entire block. Heavy weather washes the Shot
Tower's red brick, and lift St. Vincent's tent city
12 inches toward heaven.

A Collection of Odes and Descriptive Poems

In order to recognize the various ways in which odes and descriptive poems remake our perception of the world, here are a group of them.

Night (2000)
— Laure-Anne Bosselaar

wakes in bat wings
sinks into darkness
as they do

as they do
night's wings
never cast shadows

Prairie Spring (1913)
—Willa Cather

Evening and the flat land,
Rich and sombre and always silent;
The miles of fresh-plowed soil,
Heavy and black, full of strength and harshness;
The growing wheat, the growing weeds,
The toiling horses, the tired men;
The long empty roads,
Sullen fires of sunset, fading,
The eternal, unresponsive sky.
Against all this, Youth,
Flaming like the wild roses,
Singing like the larks over the plowed fields,
Flashing like a star out of the twilight;
Youth with its insupportable sweetness,
Its fierce necessity,
Its sharp desire,
Singing and singing,
Out of the lips of silence,
Out of the earthy dusk.

Windows (1992)
— Eugènio de Andrade *Translated by Alexis Levitin*

The windows
through which the brambles enter,
the trodden purple,
the smell fo the lindens, the light
slanting low,
turn this forsakenness
to devastating beauty,
without shape or form.

Wallflowers (1985)

— Cornelius Eady

Maybe they alert what's left of our animal senses.
Perhaps this is why
They arouse such an equal mix
Of pity and relief
When they walk into a room.

They inhabit the defeat that surfaces in dreams.
The powerless dreams in which our cars take us
  like crazed, possessive lovers,
Or the classrooms where we become phantom teachers, our

Lesson plans become our character flaws in neon
  across the black sky of the board.
It is the only thing the students can read.

So we watch the way we dress
And are careful of the friends we think we choose,
And when we almost stop at their seats,
It is their eyes that keep us walking,
Because deep down, neither of us can explain how
  misfortune works, what makes

It stick, what causes both of us
  to sweat as if cornered.

Detroit (2015)

—Joy Gaines-Friedler

I once photographed Coleman Young,
twenty years the mayor—he made swearing an art form,
talked in similes, said,

Racism is like high blood pressure,
the person who has it doesn't know he has it

until he drops over with a goddamned stroke.

It was the day my husband moved out
            and took his power tools with him.

That night a friend offered distraction,
two tickets to Kool and The Gang.

What have the suburbs to offer me now?
The city feels comfortable in my hand
like a found rock.

Coleman said, *Courage is one step ahead of fear.*

I think of the sound of factories in the voice
of an old boyfriend from The Cass Corridor—
cocoon of his attic bedroom, mattress on the floor,

candle light and books in that long season of snow
shining in the window—Coleman's city—

Canada faultless in the glass towers along the river.

Come on— celebrate good times...

The word *Renaissance* is painted across this city's
solid surface. The flourish hides its wounds.

Mending (1921)
— Hazel Hall

Here are old things:
Fraying edges,
Ravelling threads;
And here are scraps of new goods,
Needles and thread,
An expectant thimble,

A pair of silver-toothed scissors.
Thimble on a finger,
New thread through an eye;
Needle, do not linger,
Hurry as you ply.
If you ever would be through
Hurry, scurry, fly!
Here are patches,
Felled edges,
Darned threads,
Strengthening old utility,
Pending the coming of the new.
Yes, I have been mending ...
But also,
I have been enacting
A little travesty on life.

Untitled (C. 1810)
— Issa *Translated by Peter Beilenson*

A gate made all of twigs
with woven grass
for hinges ...
For a lock ... this snail

On Summer (1836)
— George Moses Horton

Esteville begins to burn;
The auburn fields of harvest rise;
The torrid flames again return,
And thunders roll along the skies.

Perspiring Cancer lifts his head,
And roars terrific from on high;
Whose voice the timid creatures dread;

From which they strive with awe to fly.

The night-hawk ventures from his cell,
And starts his note in evening air;
He feels the heat his bosom swell,
Which drives away the gloom of fear.

Thou noisy insect, start thy drum;
Rise lamp-like bugs to light the train;
And bid sweet Philomela come,
And sound in front the nightly strain.

The bee begins her ceaseless hum,
And doth with sweet exertions rise;
And with delight she stores her comb,
And well her rising stock supplies.

Let sportive children well beware,
While sprightly frisking o'er the green;
And carefully avoid the snare,
Which lurks beneath the smiling scene.

The mistress bird assumes her nest,
And broods in silence on the tree,
Her note to cease, her wings at rest,
She patient waits her young to see.

The farmer hastens from the heat;
The weary plough-horse droops his head;
The cattle all at noon retreat,
And ruminate beneath the shade.

The burdened ox with dauntless rage,
Flies heedless to the liquid flood,
From which he quaffs, devoid of gauge,
Regardless of his driver's rod.

Pomaceous orchards now expand

Their laden branches o'er the lea;
And with their bounty fill the land,
While plenty smiles on every tree.

On fertile borders, near the stream,
Now gaze with pleasure and delight;
See loaded vines with melons teem—
'Tis paradise to human sight.

With rapture view the smiling fields,
Adorn the mountain and the plain,
Each, on the eve of Autumn, yields
A large supply of golden grain.

Fly (2014)
— Lyn McGee

Windows for some
are walls for you.

The world says *Come on*,
the world says *Stop*,

and you listen with your eyes
mosaics of clicking beads.

Other insects are civilians
compared to you and your brisk

wringing of legs,
feet scraping brittle wings.

The disarray of rot
attracts you,

and your tongue
sops sweets.

Teach me to savor
what I find,

and how
to be precise,

catch the shifting
of shadows around me.

Fog ✱ (1919)
— Carl Sandburg

The fog comes
on little cat feet.

It sits looking
over harbor and city
on silent haunches
and then moves on.

Song to the Sugar Cane (1998)
— Virgil Suarez

At Publix today with my daughters
I spotted the green stalks of sugar cane,

tucked under the boxed Holland tomatoes,
ninety-eight cents a stalk. I grabbed the three

left and brought them home. My daughters,
born in the United States, unlike me, stand

in the kitchen in awe as I take the serrated
knife and peel away the hard green layer

exposing the fibrous white, pure slices.

"Here," I say, "nothing is ever as sweet as this."

We stand in the kitchen and chew slices
of sugar cane as I tell them this was my candy

when I was a kid growing up in Havana,
this was the only constant sweetness

in my childhood. This delicious, sweet stalk.
You chew on a piece to remember how

to love what you can't have all the time.

The Architect (2006)
— Philip Terman

A string to mark the corn seeds, secured
to a post at either end of the garden,
one of which the robin loosens, snatches,
pulls free, drags toward the cottage
she's constructing among the rose vines
tangling out of the arbor. She tugs hard,
but the other end won't give, strung
tight and tied with a double knot. Robin
imagines texture, threaded and sewn
through hay and dog hair and grass like
a garland that will reinforce, long as it takes
for the eggs to hatch, this palace. Against
resistance seizing with every exertion.
This mansion. She has all morning.

Some Writing Prompts for Odes and Descriptive Poems

1. Look at Philip Terman's poem "The Architect" above, and notice how the title is actually a metaphor for the robin in the lyric event of the poem. Write a poem in which the title is re-

defined by the poem itself, functioning as an objective correlative to the events of the poem.

2. Consider a place that you've only been to once or twice, preferably a place you haven't been in quite some time. Jot down then images you remember from those experiences—remember to consider all five senses. Now from those images construct a poem that brings that place as you remember to life.

3. Lookup some information about an animal (a strange fact, something scientific, etc.) and then write a poem that brings this animal to life, but you must incorporate this fact into the poem.

4. Find a copy of Wallace Stevens's "Thirteen Ways of Looking at a Blackbird" and look at how each of its sections functions differently (syntactically, imagistically, etc.). Now imagine something you might "see" in different ways (if it's an object you own or have, consider looking at it at different times of the day, or when you are in different moods). Write a sectional poem that engages the object in a variety of "lights" so we see it remade.

5. It's easy to write a celebratory ode to something you like quite a bit; a lot harder to write one about something you dislike. Like stories, poems get some of their energy from tension. Write a poem that celebrates something you do not like to see how to use that negative energy.

Chapter Eleven: Elegies

In the end, poetry is about nouns, it is about, as *Schoolhouse Rock* famously defined, persons, places, and things. Poetry is about what we can see, hear, smell, touch, and taste, and how those images, as delivered through words—through the best words in the best order—can generate sensations and emotions in the reader. We focused on things and places in the last chapter; now it's important to discuss people, and a poem of the person, the elegy.

We've already looked at the Lyric elegy in the form of M.L. Williams's "Hat" (page 35) and Joel Allegretti's "The Sea at Our Door" (page 57). These poets use different strategies of lyricism (one, personal; the other, observational) to capture their grief and to give a sense of the departed loved one. Williams's personal take highlights the connection between the brothers in the form of the hat, whereas Allegretti's poem enacts the emotional distancing sometimes necessary to deal with loss.

In our discussion of the narrative poem, we read Edward Arlington Robinson's "Richard Cory" (page 82). Besides telling a compact narrative about Richard Cory, it also celebrates the life of this character. Whether real or made up, Richard Cory becomes real in the poem, becomes real for the reader. The poem, therefore, functions as an elegy, a poem that celebrates "the dead." Dead, of course, doesn't have to be literal: lost loves, missing parents, personal heroes who have fallen from grace, all of these might be considered dead in some way. The *New Princeton Encyclopedia of Poetry and Poetics* says the "elegy frequently includes a movement from expressed sorrow to consolation" (322), and in doing so, the elegy fulfills part of they lyric mode's sense of ordering chaos.

Much like the ode, the traditional elegy has a form, but the contemporary elegy has evolved away from such formal trappings. In its online list of forms, the Academy of American Poets points out that "the elements of a traditional elegy mirror three stages of loss. First, there is a lament, where the speaker expresses grief and sorrow, then praise and admiration of the idealized dead, and finally consolation and solace." More recently, in the wake of Maria Ranier Rilke's famous collection *The Duino Elegies*, there is a sense that the elegy can be a meditation on death itself, on the existential grief of death's awareness, on those who have died and thus on our own mortality too.

The important thing to remember about writing the elegy, like its more prosaic cousin the obituary, is that we're celebrating an individual life, and as such, the person needs to be presented not in generic ways but in the details that engage the life and the relationship the speaker has with the "deceased." This is important for two reasons: 1. Such details honor the person, shows an attention to the details that she felt were important, and 2. such specifics allow the reader to know and invest into that relationship presented—its details about the person become the reader's details, and therefore the reader ends up having his own relationship with the elegy's subject.

Denise Low-Weso provides all the details and memories of her great-grandmother through the artifacts the woman left for the family.

The Quiltmaker (1999)

Great-grandmother Dotson,
the sodhouse settler I met once
and never forgot—
"A daughter of Isaiah and Harriet Sinks Scott
Born January 17, 1869 in Dayton, Ohio."

This rainy afternoon
I open her quilts on my bed—
Flower Garden, rosettes of white and green;
Wedding Ring, locking circles of pink;
Grandma's Fan, plumes of blue and red.

"Stricken dead after visiting all evening with friends,
Newton, Kansas, 1954."

I remember the taste of cream pie.

I remember her diary:
"I suffer today from rose fever."
"Today we have a healthy baby girl."

I look in the dresser mirror:
her quilts spread behind me
her brown eyes.

The quilts hold the essence of the great-grandmother, showing us again the power of metaphor, of the objective correlative, even in an elegy. If we think about it, we shouldn't be surprised. We associate objects with people, and often when someone dies, the loved ones want an object that represents the deceased.

This elegy functions as a personal lyric, written to capture the moment of remembering great-grandmother Dotson. What's powerful about the elegy is its ability to be written in any of the poetic modes. For instance, it's quite easy to consider "My Father Talks of 1946" (page 133) as a kind of elegy designed to keep the father's voice and story alive; ditto, "A Letter from Iceland" (page 147) could easily be a fractal exploration of a lost relationship.

A Collection of Elegies

Consider how the elegy is similar to the ode and the descriptive poem, particularly in those that are elegies for things or ideas. Notice how the poets use different techniques and strategies discussed throughout the book to write to different effects.

Elegy for my husband (2012)
— Toi Derricotte

Bruce Derricotte, June 22, 1928-June 21, 2011

What was there is no longer there:
Not the blood running its wires of flame through the whole length
Not the memories, the texts written in the language of the flat hills
No, not the memories, the porch swing and the father crying

The genteel and elegant aunt bleeding out on the highway
(Too black for the white ambulance to pick up)
Who had sent back lacquered plates from China
Who had given away her best ivory comb that one time she
    was angry
Not the muscles, the ones the white girls longed to touch
But must not (for your mother warned
You would be lynched in that all-white Ohio town you grew
    up in)
Not that same town where you were the only, the one good
    black boy
All that is gone
Not the muscles running, the baseball flying into your mitt
Not the hand that laid itself over my heart and saved me
Not the eyes that held the long gold tunnel I believed in
Not the restrained hand in love and in anger
Not the holding back
Not the taut holding

Elegy for Iain Banks (2016)
— Vince Gotera

for Iain M. Banks (1954-2013) Scottish science fiction writer known for fanciful spaceship names.

The Irish corvette Macha—a small warship—was despatched to France to bring William Butler Yeats's body home to Ireland for reburial in 1948.

Iain waits at Forth Ports in Rosyth,
where his father had once worked.
He sits on a dock, dangling his feet
into thick air over dark green water,
where once submarines lay for repair,
their blunt noses airing in dry dock.

The clipper spaceship Screw Loose,
from his novel The Player of Games,

is on the way to fetch him, to ferry him
to Avalon, Ynys Afallon, Isle of Apples,
where King Arthur reposes, braced
to save Albion—England—from peril.

Iain squints into gray, storm-clouded
sky, uncertain from which direction
Screw Loose would appear, swoop in.
A three-masted ship gracefully slips
into dock. Iain pays not one whit
of attention, still scanning the skies.

Iain is surprised when the sailing ship's
captain strides up, blue plumed tricorn
and tasseled epaulets glistening gold.
"Mr. Banks, I presume? When will you
board, sir? I am master of this vessel
to leeward of you. She is Screw Loose."

Jaw slack, Iain doesn't know what
to say. He allows himself to be led
onto the deck of the clipper ship.
Captain MacBride gives the order
to cast off, weigh anchor. The sun
emerges brightly from behind clouds.

Standing in the bow, Iain leans into
salty spray, the sea scudding and
frothing as it breaks on either side
of the clipper. Iain feels the cancer
somehow fading away, black flakes
sloughing off, flurrying away in wind.

Iain recalls how he had driven today
to the Rosyth docks in a bit of a frenzy.
He'd imagined he would be tardy and
need to sprint, yelling out for someone
to hold Screw Loose even as it left.

Or worse yet, there'd be no spaceship.

Hearing a strange metallic noise,
like a submarine klaxon dive dive,
Iain turns and looks upward
at the sails on the closest mast.
Someone in a boat alongside
the Screw Loose would have seen

Iain smile, as sails harden and shift,
drape a translucent metallic canopy
over the deck, flare '50s rocket fins.
The spaceship Screw Loose lifts
from the water and streaks smoothly
up into air, deep space, the heavens.

Elegy for Brian Wilson's Smile[1] (2016)

— George Guida

If Brian Wilson won't be happy

how will I?

When a boy of summer cries,

how will I

be Loki to Thor?

Will sounds be mine?

Will I be sound's?

Be happy I was?— or wasn't

his order, or any

or sky

or try it this way

---

[1] Brian Wilson was a founding member and the principle songwriter for the Beach Boys. Mike Love who is also mentioned in this poem is another member of the Beach Boys and continues to perform with a group as the Beach Boys.

with more with more

cherubs as castrati,

cellos, celestial saws

to

let me go home.

I feel so, you know,

let me go,

whatever you are,

my brother singing,

Linus reining lions,

stripes on televised shirts

flying mini-skirts on stage,

burning ooooooo-

eeeeeee-oooooooooooo

descending ego,

Ignoring war,

and if God only knew

why did only Carl sing?

And if Mike Love

could never love

how can I

be love, beloved, be loved?

Love can't be.

I have no books or poetry.

Just cap and beard

protect me, no Apollo

to burn the tempo,

to burnish these times.

If you ask, my answer

is a girl named "free,"

Ra humming so loud

you split your skin,

feel it break, so broke up,

every time so broke

up, so broken

the tambourines will say
that's not,
that can't,
just won't be me.

for bukowski[2] upon hearing of his death (1997)
— Lance Henson

here in paris
a small kitten purrs at the waning moon

you are gone
far from the blessed nights
where you vomited the terrorous
joy of your life

this dutch army coat smells of
cigar smoke and the yellow
clouds of dangerous sky

a man looks a long time
at the rain

some of it falls into his beer

Lion and Gin (2008)
— Dennis Hinrichsen

I pet my father like some big cat a hunter has set on the
ground,
though I am in Iowa now and not the Great Rift Valley
and what I sense as tent canvas flapping, thick with water-
proofing,

---

[2] Charles Bukowski, American poet and writer, known for his drinking and excess.

is cheap cotton
choked with starch.
Still, he is a lion on the gurney.
I talk a little to make sure he's dead.
I have some memory of riding his shoulders
through the fragrant night. Three fish coiled in a creel. So
many
butterflies
and gnats, it was two-thirds Kenya,
one-third Illinois.
And then home: the clink
of ice and gin.
And so I rub his hair, which is unwashed, and will
remain unwashed, for we will burn him.
I touch the blade of his chest.
Think of all those years I spent hovering beneath the scent of
Marlboros,
the mouthwash trace of booze; all that ice
cracking, going stale: crowned molars and mimic glaciers
fading to bled-out amber among the cuticles of lime.
Maybe that's why when he so blindly flies
on that exaltation of velocity and gas,
he doesn't linger in this world awhile as word or song,
a density we might gather round—
an aquifer, or gushing spring, as pure as gin.
Instead, he departs
as vapor.
Fragments of tooth and bone in the swept-out mass I can
throw back to dirt, or spread—a child's sugared, grainy
drink—
to water.
And now I wonder, where's the soul in this?
The agent of it?
If it un-tags, re-tags itself—a flexible, moveable,
graffiti—indelible for the time we have it,
or if it sputters on some inward cycle toward a Rubbermaid
waste bucket, sink trap ringed with cocktail residue.
As on my returning, the trays of ice were reduced to spit.

I had a drink in my hand,
that memory of riding; the fragrant night.
How can I open the freezer now and not see the milky irises of his passage;
the array of paw and pelt;
jaw wrenched so far open in that rictus of longing, gasping,
his living eyes could not help but tip and follow?

King[3] (2016)
— Kathleen A. Lawrence

B.B. beats,
Coolly canoodles
Delicious ditties
E7 etudes
Fiddling fine fugues.
Gibson guitar genuflects
Honeydew harmonicas
Insouciant instrumentals.
Jubilantly jamming,
King keenly
Loves Lady Lucille.
Mulling Mississippi, mavens
Nod 'n' nosh
On oyster's obligato, offertory of
Plectrum-plucked pearls.
Quivering quicksilver, quarter-note
River rhapsody, rhythmic
Strains of sweet shoo-fly,
Toe tapping.
Ultimate unbuttoned urbane,
Velour vinyl verses
Waxing warbled words,

---

[3] An elegy for American blues musician B.B. King in the form of an abecedarian. For more on the form, see appendix 4.

eXhaling exponentially exquisite,
Yeah yeah.
Zillions zoom zinging
Angelic arcing axe,
Boxcar bumping blues.
    B.B., take a bow.

Father's Day (2011)
— Amy Lemmon

The blue pen flows, the gospel radio brays.
This day is different from all other days.
No mass, no kaddish, everything's been said.
We'll plant a young tree with the kids instead,
right near the playground. Now we say Amen.
It's bluegrass now. A love we shared. I met
my fiddle hero at that festival,
your gig. He died just two years later: old,
a lifelong smoker. You were forty-five,
ate vegetarian and rode your bike.
Six-two, one hundred sixty pounds of brawn.
I wonder if they'll miss me when I'm gone—
the dobro twangs, the banjo taunts my ear,
the upright bass is—well, upright. Too clear.

Elegy for the Mississippi (2014)
— Travis Mossotti

It wasn't until '93, while I stood in the middle
of the shutdown interstate watching
the disemboweled Mississippi drag a farmhouse

across its breached levees,
that I understood how something as simple
and plainspoken as a river could empty the words

from its tongue and slink off
like a dog to die in the weeds.
My father stood next to me, speechless, the same man

who taught me to manage a current with a paddle,
and when that lesson failed,
how to loose a canoe

from a snag—his wedding ring slipping
off his finger as he pried us free, sank golden
into the water, into the silt.

At eighteen, I inherited a St. Louis
run dry of commerce. Powell Square gutted by its banks,
redbrick and missing teeth,

scrub tangling its tarred roof, cobblestone shores
turned into parking lots
for steamboat casinos

and floating jazz bands—this
became my American dream: rattled warehouses,
train yards, titty bars and all night discos,

Mississippi Nights and barstool whiskey poured down
my throat from the neck of a tilted bottle—
fill that empty bottle

with gasoline, stuff a rag down its throat
until it's soaked
and ready to burn.

O Captain! My Captain! (1867)
— Walt Whitman

"O Captain! My Captain! our fearful trip is done;
The ship has weather'd every rack, the prize we sought is
won;

The port is near, the bells I hear, the people all exulting,
While follow eyes the steady keel, the vessel grim and daring:
But O heart! Heart! Heart!
O the bleeding drops of red,
Where on the deck my Captain lies,
Fallen cold and dead. O Captain! My Captain! rise up and hear
    the bells;
Rise up—for you the flag is flung—for you the bugle trills;
For you bouquets and ribbon'd wreaths—for you the shores
    a-crowding;
For you they call, the swaying mass, their eager faces
    turning;
Here Captain! Dear father!
This arm beneath your head;
It is some dream that on the deck,
You've fallen cold and dead.

My Captain does not answer, his lips are pale and still;
My father does not feel my arm, he has no pulse nor will;
The ship is anchor'd safe and sound, its voyage closed and
    done;
From fearful trip, the victor ship, comes in with object won;
Exult, O shores, and ring, O bells!
But I, with mournful tread,
Walk the deck my Captain lies,
Fallen cold and dead."

Some Writing Prompts for Elegies

1. One of the obvious assignments is to write a poem for a loved one: a deceased grandmother, parent, partner, or pet. Many of the above samples are such elegies. As you write yours, make sure you give the reader an opportunity to "know" the person through the details your provide.

2. Less obvious, perhaps, is to write an elegy for someone you dislike. An elegy for a nemesis may seem counter-intuitive, but the people who antagonize us reveal a great deal about who we

are, what we believe, and how we see ourselves in the world. Think about this as you write this elegy.

3. Both Vince Gotera and Lance Henson write elegies for artists; in these cases, the subjects are both writers (Iain Banks and Charles Bukowski). Consider an artist you admire who has died and bring their work, their biography (feel free to do some research), and their influence on you into your elegy for them.

4. Not everything we memorialize in an elegy is a person. Consider what an elegy for the twentieth century might look like. Or an elegy to your adolescence. Or an animal that has recently gone extinct. Write that poem.

Chapter Twelve: Performance Poems

The performance poem is one of the trendiest poems being written today; sometimes, though, performance poetry has been reduced to a formulaic "spoken word" piece: a poem that combines personal narrative and meditation, driven more by long lines that rhyme, which are punctuated by shorter "staccato" rhymed lines. However, by reducing the definition of "performance" poems to just this presentation, such poems risk becoming more of a form (like a sonnet or a sestina) than a mode—a way of dealing with subject matter in verse.

So what do I mean when I talk about the *performance* poem? Let's face it, every poem is in some way a persona poem: in our poems, we do not usually speak the way we do with parents, co-workers, or friends at a party. Instead, we wear our poet mask. The performance poet's mask is much more akin to the one musicians, stand-up comics, and magicians wear when they take the stage. Therefore, the performance poem is written with the stage in mind. Lorca said, "Theater is poetry that rises from the book and becomes human enough to talk and shout, weep and despair" (qtd in Glazner 12). Although I think all poems are meant to be performed, the performance poem as we talk about it here, is a poem that is driven by voice, a poem in which

> When we talk about a poem's tone, we're talking about the poet's attitude toward her subject matter: annoyed with, angry, cloying, sarcastic, enamored, etc. Tone is conveyed by word choice, line break, nuance, diction, syntax, and more, and a poem can have multiple tones, just as we might have multiple attitudes toward a given subject (for example, we might love our mothers and still be sarcastic with her). Tone is a part of voice, and it needs to be nuanced and a part of the whole package. Just adding curse words, for instance, doesn't necessarily make a line sound angrier.

the writer is thinking about the oral presentation of the poem, a poem that rises to theater.

But what does it mean to have a poem that is driven by voice? By voice, we're talking about attitude; the performance poem is driven by the speaker's attitude toward the subject matter, and that's driven by the narrative, the meditation, and the sound of the words because the poet is aware that the poem is built for the page *and* the stage. The poem has to be "more alive" to the ear. But it's not just rhymes that make a poem come alive: puns, verbal play, over-the-top alliteration, and incantation can all add to the poem's attitude and remains in service to the poem's goals. The risk, always of such things, is that the verbal play obscures the poem's goal. How the poet presents it on the page also ought to reflect how it might be read aloud and clarify the poem's sharp point.

As we have said, many dramatic poems are designed to be monologues, and therefore, have some of the staged qualities of the performance poem. Unlike many lyric poems, which are designed to be private poems in a private language and to feel intimate, the performance poem is a public poem in a public language. This is why many performance poems engage social issues (as we see in Crystal Williams's poem below). Others may seem like rants or comic monologues; although such poems might *feel* like streams of consciousness, it's important to keep in mind that streams have banks, they flow toward a destination.

Lastly, sometimes performance poets write their works as prose poems (which they sometimes call "performance texts"), which require the sentences to drive the rhythm of the piece down the page.

San Francisco based Daphne Gottlieb writes a performance poem that is rich in feminist politics, sarcasm, and puns. You can see many of her performances on YouTube, but it might be better to read the poem once to yourself and then once aloud to see how you can present its tone.

watch your tense and case (1998)

oh baby
i want to be your direct object.

you know, that is to say
i want to be on the other
side of all the verbs i know
you know how to use.

i've seen you conjugate:
i touch
you touched
you heard
she knows
who cares

i'm interested in
a few decent prepositions:
above, over, inside, atop,
below, around and
i'm sure there are more
right on the tip of
your tongue.

i am ready to spend
the present perfect
splitting your infinitive
there's an art to the way you
dangle your participle and

since we're being informal it's okay to
use a few contractions, like
wasn't (going to)
shouldn't (have)
and a conjunction:
but (did it anyway)

and i'm really really glad
you're not into dependent
clauses since all i'm really
interested in is your
bad, bad grammar

and your exclamation point.

The poem's title is playful—particularly when one considers that the poem is written without capitalization! The poem's opening line begins with attitude: "oh baby." This poem is going to be a seduction: it's funny, flirty, and it uses language to its fullest performance potential: "i want to be on the other/ side of all the verbs i know/ you know how to use." The verbs that come to mind in the context of the poem are mostly sexual in nature.

The line break above on "the other" is crucial to what happens next in the poem; she plays with the conjugation of verbs and then gives us a bunch of two-word lines:

i touch
you touched
you heard
she knows
who cares

The addition of "she knows" informs us that the speaker is "the *other* woman" but doesn't care whether the guy's partner knows.

The attitude and playfulness of the poem surely come out in the last stanza with its line break on "dependent" (she obviously is an independent woman), her desire for "bad, bad grammar" (she likes bad boys) and the phallic metaphor "exclamation point." The poem's got some lyric sensibilities (its focused on this one moment of desire), it implies story, but its driving force is the voice, is its ability to be performed.

The best performance poems, obviously, are ones that allow us to hear a performance in our own head, ones in which how the poem appears on the page guides how it is presented on the stage. In order to do this, many performance poets use the page in ways similar to fractal poets: indented stanzas, spaced over sections within lines to create minor pauses, parentheticals to create an internal voice (*yeah, right*). However, unlike the post-lyric, these poems depend on not fracture, but the continuous thread of spoken thought.

A Collection of Performance Poems

By their name, we know these works are meant to not only be recited but *performed*: read aloud dynamically. As you read these, consider the tone and rhythm of the lines and consider how you would bring these poems to life on the stage.

Letter From the Water at Guantanamo Bay (2015)

— Sara Brickman

They do not want me to be a river, but I am unstoppable.
I am the perfect instrument. Capable

of every sound, but here the only sound you hear under
me is No. Is, Please. The men

in uniforms strap them to the wood
and call it water-

boarding, like drowning is an amusing summer sport.
They hood them into darkness, and tilt their heads

back, pour me up nose and throat until they can't breathe
without sucking
me in. Inside the prisoners' lungs, I see only panic,

and mothers. The men in uniforms say they do this
to get "the information."

I do not know what this "getting"
means. I only know swallow

and crush
undertow and rip-

tide. I have been
the moon's wife, but here I taste of mold

and rust.

They line me up

with their scalpels, their chains,
their American pop music

played all night
to drive the men crazy, to get the information

I do not know what desperation
feels like

but I imagine it is why the water in these men
crawls out of their eyes to say hello

Hello.

Strange, isn't it? To be 58% a thing and yet
recoil when you hear its rush—
Don't you know this? Silly human
with a dog-tag hanging round your neck,

that you are made of me? Connected
to all the humid rot in this dungeon air—

how you make a puppet of the current
in you, soldier.

How fast you make an ocean into a gutter
filled with blood and shit—

looking for answers? Like you could find an oracle
in more death

you drainers
of the heart. I made you.

Do you think the first creature crawled out of me

to invent torture?

I understand why you do this.
I know what it is
to close your eyes and see only the thousands of dead

someone has laid at your doorstep. You have filled me
with shipwreck and slave-hold but still

you holler bold
with your proud, American heart and I wish

I could stop flowing in you.

Wish I could return to the clouds,
to kiss the lightning with my wet throat

but I am locked in your muscle
as you beat each man
for praying in a language that looks

like waves. I have
one muscle,
and it wraps around the entire earth.

It is a vengeful storm
and I have learned from you how to cleave
waves from the marrow

how to lick clean.

airtight alibi... (2015)
— Monique Ferrell

today the world fell down or so the anchor woman said
her name was
heather or jane or roseanne maybe she hadn't put it just

that way and my own
rhetoric is too cataclysmic   but   we are living in trying times

in trying times she said it seems we are living several black men did very bad things today
or maybe she said and here's today's top news stories   and I heard prognosticated
the implications of color and crime   and hung my head wondering what shade
of darkness   these deeds would bring upon   my shoulders

my shoulders   bear the stain of somebody else's crime   the man who gunned his girlfriend
down   and tossed his baby out of the window   the serial rapist stalking the dog-tired bodies
of graveyard shift working women   striding the stone's throw walk from subway to home and
on the anchorwoman went knowing-it-all at me   and then the worst part of all

the worst part of all   are the expert artist sketches   that make you place a well-meaning
terrified hand to your heart   until you come to your senses reach for your phone
the villain   heather or jane or roseanne   tells you   is light skinned to medium brown

dark brown to dark skinned thin or heavyset tall or short
maybe bearded or clean shaven   and this   is too close to the bone

to the bone skin deep either of these men could have been my brother my dear friend
or the man who shares my bed I do not fear them but I fear a world that does
and so I am calling   where are you? what are you wearing today? did you see that sketch?

laughing at me they attempt to assuage my fears   but they know I'm right
know all too well   what they say   about black men in public spaces

public spaces are all we have left   the last bastion of   here is where you get to know me
that I am not a thief a batterer   a terrified fist into your seamless world   but am a man
with sisters a mother   women who turn to me for love and comfort   and because
someone loves me   I need to be seen   beyond the good intentioned craft   of an artist's pen
that imposes the bad guy's face   behind my good and safe eyes   there is no danger here

no danger here   today   as the sun sets   and all of my men are in their place
are through   the day   without being ransacked   against a subway wall   cuffed or mistaken
before a viewer's prying eyes   masculinity   still intact   for the moment   the world still sees
them as I do nothing here to see   or that   heather jane or roseanne   can say

Picasso (2015)

— Ellyn Maybe

I found a year that likes my body
1921
girl sitting on a rock
Picasso painted a woman with my thighs

walking around the museum
it hit me how Rubenesque is not just some word for
someone who likes corned beef

there I was
naked on the edge of something
overlooking water or was it salt

it was weird
nobody was screaming fat chick at the frame
nobody was making grieving sounds
but the girl in the painting looked sad
as though she knew
new eras were smudging
a forced liposuction
with rough acrylic

the caption said
girl sitting on rock

not woman who uses food to help cope
for the lack of empathy in her sphere
not the gyms are closed and there are
better muscles to develop
not girl one calorie away
from suicide
just flesh on a rock

her eyes dripping
question marks onto
girl looking into a mirror

the vibrancy
the need to chew the ice cubism
till the teeth bleed
the colors so deep
they look wet

the museum guards
watch me tentatively

I lean into the paintings

I veer to the outside
to find out what Picasso
called each work

I like titles
their vocabulary of oil

the girl on the rock
whispered to me

go girl

I love museums
call me old fashioned
but I like face to face
conversations.

The Jeffrey McDaniel Show (2000)
—Jeffrey McDaniel

I walk into a candlelit room.
All the women I've ever dated

are passing around the love poems
I gave them, and guess what?

It's the same poem—My sweet
[Put Your Name Here] if I was God

I'd make flowers smell like the back
of your neck, trees with trunks

as soft as your thighs. When we kiss
I feel like a cheerleader being crushed

to death by a giant pom-pom. Then Alex
Trebec appears. A game of Ex-

Girlfriend Jeopardy ensues.
All the categories about me.

"I'll take emotional baggage, Alex,
for twenty." "Jeffrey's mother

spanked him with this blunt object
so hard, he couldn't look in a mirror

for a week." "What's a wire hairbrush?"
"Correct, you control the board."

"Bedroom Arrogance, for thirty."
"The most narcissistic thing Jeffrey

has ever said while making love."
"What is... 'If you hold me real tight,

you can feel the centrifugal force
of the world revolving around me'?"

Should Old Shit be Forgot (2003)
— Willie Perdomo

Papo the Poet started kicking a
Poem while Dick Clark put the
City on the count

Once again we pledge down for
Whatever until the day we die
Love forever in one minute it takes
Sixty seconds to forget the one who
Left you waiting at the bust stop

And I was like:
All that shit you sayin'
Sounds good but let's

Talk about the thirty
Dollars you owe me

I hear you I hear you I hear
What you sayin'
We boys and we should
Be happy when big ass
Disco balls drop on
151 proof resolutions

Father Time says
He's only gonna smoke
On the weekends

New Year cornets
Are swept off the street
Like old friends

Champagne corks ricochet
Off bathroom walls
Roast pork burns while we
Puff and pass in project halls

Bullets kill El Barrio sky to
Celebrate holding it down
The same ole same ole shit we
Say every year
Fuck it
Pass that rum
It's cold out here
Who wants some?
You could say pleeze
You could freeze
Whatever
Happy New Years
Feliz Año Nuevo
I'm out here for a reason
Not the season

Should old shit be forgot
And all that good stuff
But I want my money
Before next year

Poem for Our Mothers (2015)
— Professor Arturo
to the students of Xavier University Preparatory School

This poem is for our mothers
This poem is for New Orleans mothers
This poem is for New Orleans women
-true believers and achievers (keepers of the faith)
who nurtured, cradled, counseled and comforted...

This poem is for the satin dolls, the yardbird suite tastes of honey,
walkin' (all by themselves) on Green Dolphin Street...
or working in steamy, hot kitchens and air-conditioned boardrooms
-on planes and trains, in banks and tanks
-at computer terminals and behind the bar
(ain't nuthin' wrong with that—she just raisin' her chirrens)

This poem is for the students of Xavier Prep
(future educators, legislators, liberators and leaders)
This poem is for Ruby Bridges, Oretha Castle Haley and Leah Chase

This poem is for the church women and the street wimmin
(Sometimes they *both*)
—Oops! My *ba-a-a-a-ad...*

This poem is for yo'momma
(Yeah, I'm talkin' 'bout yo' momma—and yo' gran'ma, too)
-yo' momma who told you 'bout sitting properly

-yo' momma who told you 'bout how hard she work
        to send you to a quality school (no thugs allowed)
-yo' momma who told you how hard it was
        when she laid down there and *had* you
-mommas who git you up off yo' offensive end
        so you can be on time for school
-momms who say "I done brought yo' behind here—and
        I'll take you away!"
-mommas who say "I'ma put so mucha you on the flo'—
        they gon' think it's the Blood Bank up in here!"
                (*them* kinda mommas)

This poem is for the mothers who see their children
                slaughtered
    in the city's mean streets
-women who cry "My baby! My baby!"
(when *it's too-oo-oo late ba-a-aby...*)

-women who say "They needs to stop all this killin'—
    I thought we had done got way mo' betta den nat!"

-women who deny themselves
    so their children can get a good education

-women who make beds to send their chirrens to school
-women who *"talk-too-much-and-worry-you-to-death"*
-women who sing *"ba-a-aby, ba-a-a-by, ba-a-a-by...)"*
-women who run for office
-women who *run* the office
-women who run *from* the office...
-women who fry chicken for a livin'
(ain't nuthin wrong with that)
-women who have you wear your clothes properly
-women who know 'bout "who shot the La-La"...

-women who tell jokes
-women who tell jokes like: "Why did the cow get a new
                house?

-because it had to *moo-oo-oove...*"

or jokes like: "Name three parts of speech –
-'My mouf, my lips, and my teefs'"

or jokes like: "What kinda rice is brown on the
outside and white
on the inside?
— 'Condoleezza Rice'"
(You *wro-o-o-ong* for that)

-women who represent
-women who *truly* represent...
-women like Mary McCleod Bethune and Sojourner Truth
-women like the African mothers who cast their children
overboard
rather than have them raised in bondage
-women who were sold at the market
-women who *shopped* at the market
-women who shopped at Schwegmann's and D.H. Holmes
-women who shopped at McKenzie's and Maison Blanche
-women who shopped at K-B and Krauss (but couldn't try
hats on)
-women who shopped at the corner sto' (mostly on creddick)
-women who shop wherever they *wan'* shop
and work wherever they *wan'* work (*after* "integration")
-women named "Elsie" (HOW NOW, BROWN COW?)
-women who sing "*That bo-o-o-o-o-oy went home to Jee-**zuss**!*"
(even though he was in that dope thang)
-women who get into that graveyard love (insteada college)
-women with sweet potato plants in their kitchen windows
-women who call you everything but "a child o' Gawd"...

-women who say things
-women who say things like: "Don't be callin' that man no
'Dawg'
That man name ain't 'Dawg'
That man name' *Mr.* Dawg'"

(Woof-woof)

or things like: "Hungry?!? – Ain't no maids in here!
You best git you summa that KARO Syrup
and a piece o' bread –
and make like it's a hamburger!"

or things like: "That boy feet done growed so fast –
he *tired* all the time."

or things like: "Boy so dumb, if he was in a hurricane he'd
say
'Why is it so windy?'"

or things like: "Boy so slow, he cain't even read his own
name
in BIG GIANT BOXCAR LETTERS!"

or things like: "Boy so dumb, he couldn't find a drink on
Bourbon Street..."

Insteada "Arab" they say "A-rabb"
Insteada "spanking" they say "whippin"
Insteada "You're a bit inebriated" they say "You tippin'"
Insteada "You're acting quite odd" they say "You trippin'"
Insteada "You're making quite a mistake" they say "You
slippin'"

This poem is for the seamstresses and the waitresses
This poem is for the teachers and the preachers
for the maids and college presidents
for the wintertime women with the summertime blues...

This is a *hurricane* poem...
This poem is for Flora, Cora, Hilda, Isabelle and Betsy
This poem is for Marilyn and Carolyn, Yolanda and Saronda
for Zelda and Emelda, for Nina and Tina
for the lovers of life and sages of their ages

for women named Aunt Sweet
for Big Momma, Gran'ma, Maw-Maw and Ma Dear
for Short Fat Fanny, Wacky Jackie and BIG GREASY NEICY
for their love hugs and Daniel Green slippers
(the *original* weapon of mass destruction)
for Doreen's Sweet Shop and Bertha's Bon Ton
for Big Shirley's and Willa Mae's Scotch House
for Fannie Mae, Annie Mae, Ida Mae, Connie Mae,
Johnnie Mae, Cora Mae, Dora Mae,
Ora Mae, Ida Mae, Jessie Mae,
Bessie Mae *(Bessie Mae Mucho-o-o-o...)*
Bay-Bay, May-May, Nee-Nay, Noo-Nay, Shantay and Ray-Ray
for Beaulah and Eulah, Nelly and Kelley
for Linda, Lydia, Leona and Lorraine
for Peola and Enola
for Brenda and Zenda (*I'm just a prisoner...*)
for the cedar robes and the chiffarobes
for Caldonia, Caldonia *(What-makes-yo'-big-haid-so-hard?)*

This poem is for Gizelle, Chanel, Creshell, Shantelle, Rochelle,
Maybelle, Annabelle and Florabelle (DING-DONG)

This poem is for Imani, Hope and Charity (where most o' y'all was born-ded)
for Khadijah and Jemima (much more than a picayune cartoon)
for Hannah, Anna, and Old Suzannah
(Don't you cry for me –
'cause I'm comin' from the Ninth Ward
with a six-pack on my knee)

for Betty, Bessy and Two-Ton Tessie
for Sharine and Jeanine *(Last Time, Last Time I Saw Jeanine...)*

for our mothers, friends, aunts, sisters, and others

-their pleasures and treasures
-their madness and badness
-their blessings and bereavement
-their challenge and achievement
-their silences and song
-their faith, everstrong
-their love like no others

This poem is for our mothers...

please let there be more than this (2015)
— Cee Williams

every poem is about my skin
(my father's skin)

septuagenarians in khakis and boat shoes
crusty women with silver puff hair
(clutched purses)

coiffed trimmings
stray cat patrol
the help is wilting

wild flowers on pressed casserole
gypsy hating pilgrims
pilgrimage to Jordan

sermon on the mound of dead indigenous
meet me where the poison ivy grows
along the shoreline dotted with mollusk shells

and pebbles
where it's safe to smoke
and watch the water, as ourselves

imagined sailors on this tiny ocean

ourselves, vacationing among the bourgeois

bluegrass lawns and pastel yellow everything
(please let there be more than this)

more than my feral world
more than chipmunk and hummingbird bliss
more than wallflower and whiskey kisses and

pocket mice acquiescing to

my skin
my father's skin, mahogany in summer,
bronze in winter

never onyx, never ebony, never tar,
never night sky void of luminous flux
in flux and fading

shades of brown and gray
my brown skin, my gray thoughts about
this place

this place
with no black cats and
not a single blade of grass misplaced

khakis
boat shoes
silver puff hairdos

pastel yellow everything

wallflower
pocket mice
poison ivy on the shoreline where

I met a gypsy and we smoked

and we sailed across a tiny ocean
to a place where we were free to be ourselves

ourselves, vacationing amongst the bourgeois
naked among pilgrims

heuristic about the world beyond
the reach of our skin.

In Search of Aunt Jemima (1995)
— Crystal Williams

I have sailed the south rivers of China and prayed to hillside Buddhas.
I've lived in Salamanca, Cuernavaca, Misawa, and Madrid, have stood
upon the anointed sands of Egypt and found my soul in their grains.

I've read more fiction, non-fiction, biographies, poetry, magazines, essays, and bullshit than imaginable, possible, or even practical. I am beyond well read, am somewhat of a bibliophile. Still, I'm gawked at by white girls on subways who want to know why and how I'm reading T.S. Eliot.

I've shopped Hong Kong and Bangkok out in heat so hot the trees were looking for shade—I was the hottest thing around. I'm followed in corner stores, grocery stores, any store.

I can issue you insults in German, Spanish, and a little Japanese.
I'm still greeted by wannabe-hip white boys in half-assed ghettoese.
I've been 250 pounds, 150 pounds and have lived and loved

every pound in between. I am still restricted by Nell Carter images of me.

I've eaten rabbit in Rome, paella in Barcelona, couscous in Morocco, and am seated at the worst table by mentally challenged Maitre'ds who think my big ass is there for coffee.

I am still passed up by cabs
passed over for jobs
ignored by politicians
guilty before innocent
Black before human.
And I'm expected to know Snoop Dog's latest hit
Mike's latest scandal
I'm expected to believe in O.J.'s innocence.
And I am still expected to walk white babies up and down 92nd street
as I nurse them, sing a hymn and dance a jig.

Sorry,
not this sista,
sista-girl, miss boo, miss it, miss thang, honey, honey-child, girl, girlfriend.

See, I am not your militant right-on sista wearing dashikis and 'fros with my fist in the air spouting Black Power while smoking weed, burning incense and making love to Shaka—formally known as Tyrone.

I am not your high-yellow saditty college girl flaunting Gucci bags and Armani suits
driving an alabaster colored Beemer with tinted windows and A.K.A. symbols rimming my license plate.

I am not your three-babies-by-fifteen, green dragon lady press on nails whose rambunctious ass is stuffed into too tight lycra with a lollipop hanging out the side of my

mouf and a piece of hair caught in a rubber band stuck to
the top of my head.

I am not your timberland, tommy hilfiger,
10K hollow-hoop wearin
gangsta rappin
crack dealin
blunt smokin
bandanna wearin
Bitch named Poochie.
I am not your conscious clearer.
I am not your convenient Black friend.
Notyourprototypenotyoursellout 'cause
massa and the big house is too good.

I am not your Aunt Jemima.
In my (8957) days of Black womanhood I've learned this:
Be careful of what you say
of what you think
of what you do
because you never know
who you're talking to.

Some Writing Prompts for Performance Poems

1. Willie Perdomo starts his poem with a fiction-like vignette: it's New Year's Eve and someone owe's him money. Consider a story that can launch you into a meditation.

2. Many performance poems engage social and political subject matter. They are public poems in a public language after all. Consider how Crystal Williams and Monique Ferrell engage the issue of race relations and the African American experience in their poems in ways that are both personal and public. Consider a subject you can engage on those two levels.

3. Performance poems use a variety of techniques to create momentum in recitation. Look again at "Poem for the Mothers"

and “In Search of Aunt Jemima”; now write a poem in which anaphora and incantation lead the poem down the page to create what at first glance might seem like a rant.

Chapter Thirteen: Final Thoughts

By now you've experimented with a variety of modes in which the poem thinks about your subject matter, and you've learned about craft along the way. Now it's time for you to take what you've learned and use that to help you find your voice, to write the poems not only that you want to write, but that you need to write, are perhaps meant to write.

This book isn't meant to be comprehensive; rather it is meant to be foundational. Luke Howard's classification of clouds was a start to something. He also realized that many clouds possess attributes of more than one cloud type; thus the nimbo-cumulus cloud was created—one that showed hallmarks of both the nimbus and cumulus clouds. So, too, we might think of poems as sharing attributes of more than one mode: for example, the lyric-meditation might be a meditation composed of various lyric segments with little narrative. A lyric-narrative might have slightly less story than the traditional narrative, avoiding some of the elements of fiction (a good example of this is Lee Ann Roripaugh's "Innocence" on page 83, which opens with a childhood story of getting up to see the moon landing, but ends without a resolve to the initial story). The classifications above have deliberately fuzzy boundaries.

Knowing the different modes, the different ways poems engage and enact our thinking, allows us to better see what types of poems fit our personalities and our subject matter. Knowing that our thinking is a pathway for the reader's access into the poem, and that we shape this thinking through the process presented on the page (from line length to poem length, from figurative language to narrative strategy), helps us consider the various potentialities of the page. It also helps to guide what sorts of revisions we might consider in order to improve subsequent drafts of a poem.

Revision is where the work of being an artist gets done. Moving lines/stanzas from one place to another, playing with diction, replacing metaphors ... all these things and more are part of the process of taking early drafts of a poem and making them art. Your classmates and teachers, of course, help by making suggestions, but there are times when you don't have someone to look over your work with you. Ask yourself: *what is the poem trying to do? Is this the best mode of doing it? Why? What are the poem's strengths? Weaknesses?*

Remember: it's always good to be open to possibilities. Sometimes a poem may fail because what we're trying to do isn't suited to the subject. A three page meditative poem might not be working, but seven of its lines might make for a strong lyric poem. Take the lyric poem and run. The rest, leave on the cutting room floor.

Appendices

Appendix 1: The Five Tool Poet

The first tool is the centrality of lyricism. By lyric, we mean a personal stance that conveys the ecstatic—that experience of being taken out of ourselves (emotionally, spiritually, sexually, psychologically, artistically, etc.); one might say there are five main rhetorical modes to express such moments:

a. **Lyric**: Lyric poems capture the lyric event, often a small moment, without much (or any) story at all. The poem engages only the sensibility of the "event." As Kenneth Koch says "the point may only be to get into that poem the look of a locust tree in the early spring."

b. **Narrative**: Narrative poems tell stories, often the story of the lyric event.

c. **Meditative**: Meditative poems reflect upon the significance of the lyric event while making connections to the narrative process of the lyric experience, other experiences, and the illustrations of abstract thought.

d. **Dramatic**: In the dramatic or persona poem, the author employs the personal stance of a character, fictive or realistic, and the poem concerns itself with a lyric event that is personal to that adopted persona.

e. **Fractal**: The fractal poem (or post-lyric poem) formally enacts the fractured nature of the lyric experience rather than trying to order it, allowing the poem to be fragmented.

The second tool is an awareness of the image's central importance to poetry. As stated earlier, image goes beyond mere description to communicate an experience or feeling so vividly that it enters the readers' minds and allows readers to have the sensations themselves. At the foundational level, imagery engages the five senses; let's consider the ways the poem and sensory imagery interact.

Visual Imagery: Visual descriptions are the most common descriptions we encounter.

Olfactory Imagery: It is often said that smells can conjure the most powerful of memories. Descriptions of smells can stimulate the readers' own sense of smell while reading, as in these lines about a campsite:

Last night's charred logs still smolder, water wet,
gaggingly damp, and the old beer smell returns
more quickly than language. Coffee cologne
tells you someone has the camp stove going.
The smell of bacon smoke confirms it. Last night,
a rank memory of ugly talk on your breath.

Auditory Imagery: We live in a world of sounds, and poems can bring the world to life. Consider the role of onomatopoeia in reenacting the sonic world around us; think of the sounds syllables make. Listen to how these lines bring a county fair to life:

Pop! WOOwooWOOwoo wails a siren
followed by *Winner, we have a winner* crackling
above the clown heads. *Nooo*, a boy whines. No
silence thanks to the **thump thump thump** of electronic
music. And in counter rhythm, the roller coaster
clack-clack-clack-clack-clacking skyward.

Taste Imagery: We all have a favorite meal or a taste that gets us licking our lips, but not all tastes are food tastes. We can taste our tears. We can taste a snowflake by standing outside and catching one on the tongue. With its thousands of taste buds on the surfaces of its papillae, the tongue provides an opportunity to write about the flavors of the world. Consider how Elizabeth Alexander does it in these lines from "Butter":

... Growing up
we ate turkey cutlets sauteed in lemon
and butter, butter and cheese on green noodles,
butter melting in small pools in the hearts
of Yorkshire puddings, butter better
than gravy staining white rice yellow,
butter glazing corn in slipping squares,
butter the lava in white volcanoes
of hominy grits, butter softening
in a white bowl to be creamed with white
sugar, butter disappearing into
whipped sweet potatoes, with pineapple,

butter melted and curdy to pour
over pancakes, butter licked off the plate
with warm Alaga syrup.

Tactile Imagery: These images engage touch or being touched with descriptions that allow the reader to imagine it, often driven by verbs and metaphor as in "when she bent to inhale the rose,/ the silky petals tickled her nose" or in "the sleet on her unscarfed cheeks/stung like black flies."

Flat out description though is only one way to bring imagery to life; figurative language can also enhance the power of our images. The five most common types of figurative language are synesthesia, synechdoche, metonymy, simile, and metaphor.

Synesthesia: This is the employment of words and terms normally associated with one sense being used in regards to another. We see the pronounced use of synesthesia in these lines:

Neon screams from inside the bar
and the bartender's smile tastes like home cooking
in a home you didn't grow up in

but wanted to. A whole childhood spent eating
a father's cayenne silence, mother's cotton candy
praise. Here even the juke box songs sparkle.

We all know neon lights don't "scream." And although a person's mouth might taste like something they've eaten or drank, we know silence isn't "cayenne" nor do jukebox songs "sparkle." By using words associated with one sense to another, we create tension and surprise that helps deepen the experience of language.

Simile: A figure of speech in which an explicit comparison is made between two essentially unlike things, usually using "like," "as," or "than."

Metaphor: A figure of speech in which a word or phrase denoting one object or idea is applied to another, thereby suggesting a likeness or analogy between them. While most metaphors are nouns, verbs can be used as well to create metaphoric connections as in these lines from Shelley's "The Clouds":

Till the calm rivers, lakes, and seas,
Like strips of the sky fallen through me on high,
Are each **paved** with the moon and these.

Synecdoche and *metonymy*: These two figures of speech are very similar. Synecdoche allows for a part of the whole to represent the whole, as when you say "I got a new set of wheels" instead of "a new car." Metonymy, on the other hand, is a figure of speech in which you call something the name of an associated object, as when you call a mercenary "a hired gun" or you call a king or queen "the crown."

The third tool of poetry involves one's attention to language. Samuel Coleridge said poetry is the best words in the best order, for poetry isn't just about the words we use, but also about how we string those words together; therefore, it's good to consider all the aspects of usage.

Syntax: The way in which words and phrases are arranged in grammatical structures; poetic syntax sometimes departs from conventional usage and grammar. Changing diction creates emphasis, generates tone, and transforms how the reader experiences the poem's language. There is a big difference between saying "They are cute" and "Cute they are."

Diction: The choice of words, phrases, sentence structures, and figurative language in a literary work; the manner or mode of verbal expression, particularly with regard to clarity and accuracy. The diction of a poem may range from colloquial to formal, from literal to figurative, from concrete to abstract.

Connotation: The suggestion of a meaning by a word beyond what it explicitly denotes or describes. The words "house" and "home," for instance, both mean the place where one lives, but by connotation, "home" also suggests security, family, love, and comfort.

Denotation: The literal dictionary meaning(s) of a word as distinct from an associated idea or connotation. Many words have more than one denotation, such as the multiple meanings of "fair" or "spring." In ordinary language, we strive for a single precise meaning of words to avoid ambiguity, but poets often take advantage of multiple meanings to suggest more than one idea with the same word.

The fourth tool of a poet involves attention to the sounds of the spoken poem. The nature of sonic resources used by poets conveys and can reinforce meaning through the skillful use of sound. The devices that contribute to the creation of sonic interplay include alliteration, assonance, consonance, rhyme (including internal rhyme, half-rhyme), onomatopoeia, cacophony, rhythm, and meter.

Alliteration: We often associate alliteration with tongue twisters. It refers to the repetition of the initial sounds (usually consonants) of stressed syllables in neighboring words or at short intervals within a line or passage, as in "wild and woolly," or the L sounds in this line from Shelley's "The Cloud": "I bear light shade for the leaves when laid."

Alliteration can have a gratifying (or grating!) effect. It can give reinforcement to stresses, and can serve as a subtle connection or emphasis of key words, but alliterated words should not call attention to themselves by strained usage.

Assonance: The repetition of similar vowel sounds in syllables ending with different consonant sounds, as in "roof," "tooth," and "shoot."

Consonance: The repetition of consonant sounds within a poem, wherever they appear in a word, as in the K sounds in this sentence: "It was **c**lear Ri**ck**y's **c**at was o**k**ay after we too**k** it to Do**c**tor O'**C**onnor."

End rhyme: The type of rhyme we most associate with poetry, it is rhyme that happens at the end of two lines of poetry, as in these lines from William Blake's "London":

I wander through each chartered street,
Near where the chartered Thames does flow,
And mark in every face I meet
Marks of weakness, marks of woe.

Internal rhyme: A rhyme occurring inside a line. The rhyme may be with words within the line but not at the line's end, or it may be with a word within the line and a word at line's end, as in Shelley's "The Cloud": "I bring fresh **showers**, for the thirsting **flowers**."

Half-rhyme: Also called approximate rhyme, slant rhyme, off rhyme, imperfect rhyme, or near rhyme, it is a rhyme in which the sounds are similar, but not exact, as in "home" and "come" or "close" and "lose." Most near rhymes are types of consonance.

Cacophony: Discordant sounds in the jarring juxtaposition of harsh letters or syllables which are grating to hear, sometimes used in poetry for effect. The use of words with the consonants B, K and P, to cite one example, produce harsher sounds than the soft F and V or the liquid L, M and N.

Rhythm: An essential of all poetry, rhythm is the regular or progressive pattern of recurrent accents in a poem's flow/

- In free verse (the prevailing poetic of contemporary and twentieth century poets), rhythm is dependent on the syllabic cadences emerging from the poem's diction and context.
- In classical verse (the prevailing poetic through the nineteenth century), this is determined by the use of "metrical feet."

Meter: A measure of rhythmic quantity.

- In free verse, meter distinguishes between the frequency and placement of accented and unaccented syllables that emerge from the diction and context of the poem.
- In classical verse, the unit of meter is the foot and metrical lines are named for the type and number of feet in each line: monometer (1), dimeter (2), trimeter (3), tetrameter (4), pentameter (5), hexameter (6), heptameter (7), and octameter (8); thus, a line containing five iambic feet, for example, would be called iambic pentameter. Other types of feet include the trochee, spondee, anapest, and dactyl. **For more on meter, see appendix 2.**

The last tool of the poet's trade is an attention to form and structure. Because verse defies the traditional prosaic phrasing of paragraph, form and structure become especially important to its experience. First and foremost, poems are written in lines, and attention to the line affords a variety of strategies for the poet to manipulate meaning, sound play and more. (**For more on the line, see appendix 3.**) To create a form and structure that supports (or is at odds with) the contents of the poem, a variety of craft devices are manipulated, including repetition and incantation (anaphora), line, stanza, enjambment, end-stopping, and the sentence's relationship to those things.

Repetition/Incantation: A highly effective unifying force, the repetition of sound, syllables, words, syntactic elements, lines, stanzaic forms, and metrical patterns establishes cycles of expectation which are reinforced with each successive fulfillment. The repetition of opening words or phrases of a line is called *anaphora.*

Line: The primary unit of meaning in a poem.

- The line is fundamental to poetry, as it is the distinguishing factor between prose and verse.
- In metrical verse, line lengths are determined by genre or convention, as well as by meter. Otherwise, and especially in free verse, a poet can give emphasis to a word or phrase by isolating it in a short line.
- When reciting poems, the line-end signals for a slight pause, the time it takes for your eyes to return to the left margin.
- The traditional practice of capitalizing the initial line-letters contributes to the visual perception of the line as a unit; this practice is often not observed in modern free verse.

Stanza: A division made by arranging the lines into units separated by a space. A poem with stanzas of regular length is described as having a stanzaic form, but not all verse is divided in stanzas (the poem is the stanza).

The regularity of stanza patterns conveys an impression of order and the expectation of closure. That said, there may be no line groupings or irregular line groupings similar to paragraphs of prose.

Enjambment: The act of breaking a line without any punctuation so that the rhythm rushes the reader from the end of one line to the beginning of the next without pause.

End-stopping: A line of verse in which a logical or rhetorical pause occurs at the end of the line, usually marked with a period, comma, semicolon, or other punctuation.

Look at Bruce Weigl's "What Saves Us" (page 71) for a study in line endings. The first half of the poem uses enjambment to capture the breathlessness of the scene, whereas the second half of the poem is slowed by the number of end-stopped lines to enact the fear of death.

Appendix 2: On Meter

Many students struggle with the notion of meter because they can't hear where to put stresses in words and phrases. Unlike song, where the beat is emphasized by the rhythm section, when we read poems, more often than not, no one plays a snare drum behind us to clarify where the beat should go. To make it more complicated, much of how we pronounce words differ due to regionalisms.

What we need to know is that syllables are either emphasized or de-emphasized when we speak them. For instance, we don't say **in**side, rather we say in**side**: the latter syllable gets more stress naturally than the former. This would be demarcated above the two syllables like so: ˇ ˊ . This pattern of an unstressed syllable followed by a stressed one is called an iamb. A combination of such syllables into patterns is called *a foot.*

In a sentence we tend not to stress articles, conjunctions, and prepositions as much as we do nouns and verbs. In the following sentence one might see how this plays out: The **cat** and **dog fought** in the **li**ving **room**. The more important words/sounds get emphasized slightly more than the others.

Traditional verse works with meter: the sonnet, for instance, is written in iambic pentameter, which means a meter of five iambs: *In**side** the **house** my **son** was **play**ing **games**.* Not every poem written in iambic pentameter though has a lockstep rhythm: that would get boring. If we look again at this sentence: *The **cat** and **dog fought** in the **li**ving **room***, we see that this is also a five beat line, four of the five feet coming in the form of iambs. The middle foot (**fought** in) has the stressed syllable come first. This rhythmic pattern is called a trochee (annotated like this: ˊ ˇ).

Here is a list of metrical types with examples.

Iamb	unstressed stressed	a**gain**
Trochee	stressed unstressed	**dy**ing
Spondee	stressed stressed	**dumptruck**
Pyrrhic	unstressed unstressed	into
Anapest	unstressed unstressed stressed	in the **room**
Dactyl	stressed unstressed unstressed	**care**fully

When we scan a poem for meter, the annotation works as such: ʹ above the syllable means it's stressed and ˇ means it's unstressed.

Understanding meter can be hard, for it's not an exact science. There are some schools of thought that include a half stress (denoted by reversing the stress mark like so ` above the syllable). Another school of thought believes there are five degrees of stress. All of this suggests that as language has evolved and poetry has gotten further from the strictures of strict meter, our understanding of how we stress syllables has changed. At the early stages of writing poetry, it's important to acknowledge that not every syllable we speak has the same force, and that "tone" is often affected when we stress syllables differently (for example, we might say every syllable more forcefully when we are angry).

Suffice to say, it's important to recognize that even if you're not going to write in fixed forms, paying attention to the *cadence* of the sentence in terms of its rhythmic and musical qualities is an important aspect of free verse. Too many unstressed syllables in a line can make the poem feel sluggish or less dynamic in places. Too many stressed syllables in a row can be difficult to say. Being aware that words not only have sounds but that we say those sounds with relative pressures is an important aspect to hearing poems and making meaning. Scanning your poems just to hear what syllables are stressed is a good way to ensure the tautness of your lines.

Appendix 3: Rookeries and Red Wheelbarrows: Some Thoughts on the Poetic Line

What makes a poem a poem? Well, we all accept that a poem is written in lines, rather than sentences, but what does that mean for us as poets? Where do lines "break" and who breaks them? The phrase makes it so accidental, when really line is one of the most deliberate of our choices. Before the advent of free verse, lines were often decided by meter and rhyme; in the contemporary era, poets often need to decide what drives their line, poem by poem. Writing in lines allows a poet to manipulate the pacing of the poem, the meaning of the poem, and the rhythm of the poem.

Here's a famous poem by William Carlos Williams:

> So much depends
> upon
>
> a red wheel
> barrow
>
> glazed with rain
> water
>
> beside the white
> chickens.

If we were to just write this out as a sentence, "So much depends upon a red wheel barrow glazed with rain water beside the white chickens," it would be unimpressive. Fortunately, we're not writing sentences; we're writing poems, so maybe we should make it look like a poem. Here it is as a quatrain:

> So much depends upon
> a red wheel barrow
> glazed with rain water
> beside the white chickens.

Perhaps this is more interesting, but not overly so. The question is, why? Why does the poem as Williams published it *work* in ways that it doesn't work as a sentence or a quatrain?

The simple answer: the line and stanza.

The line in this poem brings a syncopated jazz beat to the dull farm implement:

So **much** de**pends**
u**pon**

a **red wheel**
bar**row**

glazed with **rain**
water

be**side** the **white**
chickens.

As published, the two stressed syllables in the first line of each stanza and the single stressed syllable of each second line, give the poem a jazzy rhythm which works against the pastoral, farm imagery of the scene. Since the two beats in the opening lines never occur in the same place, they have a less metronomic sensibility than we associate with metrical poetry.

But also consider the look of a wheelbarrow. It has a bucket and a two handles, with a wheel at the center of it. Notice how each stanza kind of looks like a wheel barrow.

Line, then, becomes defining for the poem, and it can be transformational. Poets use line and stanza to create and manipulate the reader's experience of the language. For example, in this exercise, I asked students for four lines. Students volunteered the lines one at a time:

I like penguins.
They are so cute
in their tiny tuxedos
like a thousand James Bonds.

Like the Williams poems, these lines are pretty dull as far as their phrasing is concerned. What are they really? A declarative sentence, a declarative sentence, a prepositional phrase and a simile. The diction doesn't do much for the poem, except in the second line in which the "so" makes this poem sound as if written by a middle school student: "they are *so* cute." But look what happens if we alter the syntax of the second line:

I like penguins.
So cute they are
in their tiny tuxedos
like a thousand James Bonds.

By changing the word order, the second line now sounds like it is using some "high" diction (one of my students called it "Yoda" talk), giving the poem a seriousness that isn't conveyed with the subject matter.

Of course, in the current order, we know exactly what the poet is talking about. What happens though, if we swap the order of the first and last lines so that we begin with the simile:

Like a thousand James Bonds
they are so cute
In their tiny tuxedos.
I like penguins.

In this version the poem begins with mystery. By beginning with the pop-cultural reference of James Bonds, we begin with questions for the reader: what are like a thousand James Bonds? And how are they like a thousand James Bonds? We don't get the answer. The writer may have piqued our curiosity enough that we continue downward, as opposed to the first version where, if we don't like penguins, or we think penguins have been over-done, we may not have continued.

Furthermore, consider what happens were we to reverse the syntax of that new last line:

Like a thousand James Bonds
they are so cute
In their tiny tuxedos.
Penguins I like.

Now we end on the speaker's liking as opposed to the vision of the penguins that ends the previous version.

We can swap the order another way:

They are so cute,
like a thousand James Bonds—
I like penguins
in their tiny tuxedos.

Again, we delay the object of the speaker's affection: what is so cute? What are like a thousand James Bonds? The third line—the declarative line—answers those questions and then is followed up with the expository final line. The connotation of *tuxedos* is dramatically different than that of the other alternative endings: as tuxedos makes us think of formal occasions. Although James Bond sometimes wears a tux, ending on Bond surely doesn't only bring that connotation into the poem.

By only reversing line order and word order, we create a variety of possible options for this poem that change how the reader experiences penguins and the speaker's sense of the bird. Now consider what happens if we change the length of the lines.

I like
penguins. They are
so cute in their tiny tuxedos
like a thousand
James Bonds.

By breaking the first line on "like" we hold a pause on the word, emphasizing the emotion of "liking." The next line is an affirmation of the beingness of penguins. Look how the middle line is the longest line, and it's "book-ended" by the **s-o/o-s** sound combination. The fourth line makes us wonder a thousand what? A thousand bucks? *James Bonds* is surely not what we're expecting.

This version of the poem is doing something interesting in terms of rhythm, too. The first and last lines are both two-syllable lines. The second and fourth lines are both four syllable lines, so that the poem mirrors itself.

Some slight shifts change how we read it even more:

I
like penguins
in their tiny tuxedoes.
Like a thousand
James Bonds. They are
so cute.

The pauses inherent in the line breaks make the second line *like penguins* seem like a simile. It isn't, but it changes how we experience everything that follows. By using a bit of counter point in the penultimate line: *James Bonds they are*, our eye reads that they are James Bonds because our eyes are trained to work independently of our ears—so even though our ears hear the sentences as they are punctuated, our eyes see the patterns of words that each line is independently as well as a whole.

Change it up just a bit more and you get, what is to me, perhaps the most interesting of these poems:

I
like penguins—
like a thousand James Bonds
they are
so cute in their tiny tuxedos.

The second and third lines seem to create a pattern of similes: *I'm like penguins, I'm like a thousand James Bonds...* that force us to consider how these things are similar, how they might be similar to the speaker and establish an anaphoratic pattern that is instantly broken by line four *they are* (the simile of course remains accurate—we all "are"), but the sentence and line are doing different things—the way they ought to.

So far such line alterations have resulted in a "longer" poem because the number of lines is longer, so consider the second version in only three lines:

I like penguins. So cute
they are in their tiny tuxedoes
like a thousand James Bonds.

In this variation of the poem, line one isn't just a declarative line of taste—instead *so cute* answers the natural *why*/the reader might ask. Furthermore, line two forces us to *see* the penguins by pointing them out in a full independent clause. The last line, of course, is a pure simile, and adds, as it always has, a bit of humor in the pop cultural reference. Are these the Sean Connery James Bonds or the Timothy Dalton James Bonds or the terrible aging Roger Moore James Bonds? There are a thousand of them—like the end scene of the original *Casino Royale*.

Realize, I'm working only with the same original set of sixteen words. Imagine the possibilities of repeating just one word:

> I like penguins.
> They are so cute. Penguins
> in their tiny tuxedos
> like a thousand James Bonds.

The addition of the word *penguins*—both times at the end of a line—emphasizes the presence of the penguins. Don't forget there are "thousands" of them.

Or consider one of the variations above with the additional "penguins."

> They are so cute,
> like a thousand James Bonds—
> penguins. I like penguins
> in their tiny tuxedos.

By changing *I like penguins* to *penguins. I like penguins* we reinforce the liking of penguins in the line, even though the first "penguins" belongs to the previous sentence. And if you end with that line:

> Like a thousand James Bonds
> in their tiny tuxedos
> they are so cute.
> Penguins. I like penguins.

The last line repeats *penguins*. Once as a fragment. Then as a declarative sentence. How does the fragment change the tone of the declarative sentence at the end? The first use of *Penguins* answers all our questions, but with a dumbfounded bluntness, thus giving the final sentence a kind of wistfulness as if the speaker knows it's silly to like penguins so much.

If this is what can be done with four lines—four fairly mundane and ultimately uninteresting lines—then imagine what can be done with your own lines should you actually choose to spend time considering the limitless possibilities of line length and diction, tone and sound. The line, we're reminded, is the core of poetry—not the sentence. We make and manipulate meaning through how we make and manipulate line. And by looking once more at "The Red Wheelbarrow" we see the further possibilities stanza might afford us.

Ultimately, creating rules for our line is the one way we make meaning in the poem, one way we create the rules for a tennis court without the net. Line might be dictated by meaning or sentence or rhythm or rhyme. I like to think of the line as a series of rubber bands. How far can they stretch out before they snap us back to the left margin? The poem's energy is in the motion back, the slight hesitancy of whatever lingers at the end of one line and the jarring point we return to.

Appendix 4: A (Very) Brief Discussion of Traditional Form

As I've said elsewhere, there are plenty of books about poetic forms out there, and many students have learned about some of them, such as the sonnet, in literature classes, so I don't spend much time on the structures of fixed forms in this book. However, because several of the sample poems in these pages exemplify traditional forms, what follows is a quick guide to some of the more popular ones.

Abecedarian: This is an acrostic poem, meaning a poem in which something is "spelled" down the left hand margin; in the case of the abecedarian, each line begins with the next letter of the alphabet.

Ghazal: A Persian form, the ghazal, according to the *Longman Anthology of Poetic Terms*, is "composed of five to twelve couplets, the last of which contains the author's name" (this is particularly ironic because the sample it gives doesn't have the author's name in it!). The theme in each couplet echoes each other, and some writers take this to mean that there is a refrain phrase at the end of each couplet.

Haiku: A form most of you probably already know, the haiku is a short, imagisitcally vibrant Japanese poem of three lines/seven-teen syllables, most often described as having five syllables in the first line, seven in the second, and five again in the third. It is suggested that the third line "turn" in someway from the logic of the first two lines.

Pantoum: As in the villanelle, whole lines are repeated, but in the pantoum the whole poem is composed of repeating lines, creating a chainlink effect that comes full circle. Made up of quatrains (four-line stanzas) with a rhyme scheme that has the stanza's odd-numbered lines rhyme, and its even-numbered lines rhyme, the challenge is that the second and fourth lines of stanza one become the first and third lines of stanza two; the new second and fourth lines of stanza two become lines one and three of stanza three, etc. The poem ends with either a couplet (lines two and four of the next-to-last stanza become the closing couplet) or a quatrain which brings back of the first and third lines of the poem as the final stanza's second and fourth line.

Sestina: A 39-line poem featuring six six-line stanzas (sestets) and a closing tercet, the poem repeats the six end words of the first sestet in a revolving pattern throughout the other stanzas. In the final tercet, three are repeated internally and three at the end lines. The pattern follows:

stanza 1	stanza 2	stanza 3	stanza 4	stanza 5	stanza 6
word 1	word 6	word 3	word 5	word 4	word 2
word 2	word 1	word 6	word 3	word 5	word 4
word 3	word 5	word 4	word 2	word 1	word 6
word 4	word 2	word 1	word 6	word 3	word 5
word 5	word 4	word 2	word 1	word 6	word 3
word 6	word 3	word 5	word 4	word 2	word 1

In the tercet, the end words are either set up as words 1, 3, and 5 or words 5, 3, and 1 with the other words appearing one in each of the lines.

Sonnet: Perhaps the most familiar verse form, a sonnet is composed of fourteen lines in iambic pentameter, with a fixed rhyme scheme. The rhyme pattern changes based on whether the poem is a Shakespearean sonnet, a Petrarchan sonnet, or a Miltonian sonnet. More contemporary sonnets may avoid these three rhyme schemes altogether to create a rhyming pattern of their own (David Wojahn does this wonderfully in his book *Mystery Train*).

Villanelles: The villanelle is a French form composed of nineteen lines, two of which repeat often, and rhymes that go as follows:

Stanza 1	Stanza 2	Stanza 3	Stanza 4	Stanza 5	Stanza 6
Line 1A	A	A	A	A	A
Line 2B	B	B	B	B	B
Line 3A	Line 1A	Line 3A	Line 1A	Line 3A	Line 1A
					Line 3A

This requires the poet to find a good deal of rhyming/half-rhyming words; it also requires that the first and third line can be repeated in such a way as to make them seem different each time we encounter it. More and more, poets don't repeat the whole line but rephrase it slightly or repeat just the latter half of the line.

Of course there are numerous other traditional forms: rondeaus, cinquains, haibun, ballads, and so much more. A good book of forms (see appendix 5) will help you explore the possibilities of formal verse.

Appendix 5: Additional Reading

As I've said numerous times, there are plenty of books out there to teach you about craft, to give you writing prompts, to get you thinking about the poem in a variety of ways. Here are few favorites with some words about what they offer.

Addonizio, Kim and Dorianne Laux. *The Poet's Companion.* NY: WW Norton, 1997.

This is a top notch guide to generating content, broadening the way we think of subject matter, and how to work with aspects of craft including image, form, and sound play. It comes with lots of writing prompts, revision strategies, and advice for the writing life.

Arp, Thomas R. and Greg Johnson. *Perrine's Sound and Sense: an Introduction to Poetry.* Boston: Thomson Wadsworth, 2005.

Since its introduction when Perrine himself wrote it over 60 years ago, this has been a tried and true guide to the basic elements of poetic craft.

Behn, Robin and Chase Twichell. *The Practice of Poetry: Writing Exercises from Poets who Teach.* NY: Quill, 1992.

One of the quintessential collections of poetry prompts by teacher-poets followed by a discussion of the art of revision.

Caplan, David. *Poetic Form: an Introduction.* NY: Pearson Longman, 2007.

The title says it all: this is a book that focuses on many of the major poetic forms of the Western tradition, but it's not nearly comprehensive as some other books on the subject.

Davis, Todd and Erin Murphy. *Making Poems. Forty Poems with Commentary by the Poets.* Albany: SUNY Press, 2010.

A good to the process of making a poem as a poem is presented followed by the story of its genesis. It demystifies the process of writing poems by allowing the reader the opportunity to "look behind the curtain."

Drury, John. *Creating Poetry.* Cincinnati: Writer's Digest Books, 1991.

This is a well-written guide to the basics of prosody (form, meter, figurative language, etc.).

Goodman, John. *Poetry Tools and Technique.* British Columbia: Gneiss Books, 2011.

A simple, smart, inexpensive guide to the techniques of poetry. Bare bones and clear, this book is a terrific desk reference for considering various aspects of craft.

Kooser, Ted. *The Poetry Home Repair Manual: Practical Advice for Beginning Poets.* Lincoln: U Nebraska Press, 2005.

A bit homespun but well done, this book focuses on finding subject matter and getting words down on the page while giving encouragement and prodding novice writers to take chances.

Minar, Scott. *The Working Poet II.* Dubois, PA: MAMMOTH Books, 2013.

Half of this book presents writing prompts from a variety of teaching poets; the other half is an anthology of contemporary poetry. A good book if you're looking for work generating assignments.

Myers, Jack. *The Portable Poetry Workshop.* Boston: Thomson Wadsworth, 2005.

A discussion of poetic "formulae" in terms of how to structure the poems you write, with further discussion of form, prosody, and structure.

Strand, Mark and Eavan Boland. *The Making of a Poem.* NY: WW Norton, 2000.

This is a fine guide to the majority of major traditional forms in the European tradition, with discussions and sample poems.

Works Cited

"Elegy: Poetic Form." Academy of American Poets. https://www.poets.org/poetsorg/text/elegy-poetic-form. Online.

Fulton, Alice. "Fractal Amplifications: Writing in Three Dimensions." *Thumbscrew* 12 (Winter 1998–99). http://www.poetrymagazines.org.uk/magazine/record.asp?id=12199. Online.

Glazner, Gary Mex. *Poetry Slam: The Competitive Art of Performance Poetry*. San Francisco: Manic D Press, 2000. Print.

Hsieh, Liu. *The Literary Mind & The Carving of Dragons*. Trans. Vincent Yu-Chung Shih. New York: NYRB, 2015. Print.

James, D.G. *Scepticism and Poetry*. London: George Allen & Unwin, 1937. Print.

John, Eileen. "Poetry and Directions for Thought." *Philosophy and Literature* 37,2 (October 2013). 451–471. Print.

Joyce, James. *Portrait of the Artist as a Young Man*. Hertfordshire: Wordsworth Editions, 1992. Print.

Kirby, David. *Writing Poetry: Where Poems Come From and How to Write Them*. Boston: The Writer, Inc, 1997. Print.

Koch, Kenneth and Kate Ferrell. *Sleeping on the Wing: An Anthology of Modern Poetry with Essays on Reading*. New York: Vantage Books, 1982. Print.

Muldoon, Paul. *The End of the Poem*. New York: Farrar, Straus, Giroux, 2006. Print.

Myers, Jack and Michael Simms. *The Longman Dictionary of Poetic Terms*. New York: Longman, 1989. Print.

Orr, Gregory. *Poetry as Survival.* Athens: U Georgia Press, 2002. Print.

Pratt, William. *The Imagist Poem.* New York: Plume, 1963. Print.

Preminger, Alex and T.V.F. Brogan. *The New Princeton Encyclopedia of Poetry and Poetics.* Princeton: Princeton U Press, 1993. Print.

VanCleave, Ryan and Chad Prevost. *Breathe: 101 Contemporary Odes.* Chattanooga: C&R Press, 2008. Print.

Wallas, Graham. *The Art of Thought.* London: Jonathan Cape, 1926. Print.

Index of Poets and Titles

"airtight alibi" 197
Ali, Abdul 144
Allegretti, Joel 57
"Along the River Palms" 111
"Alzheimer's" 58
Anderson, Alice 99
"Apartment" 109
"The Architect" 174
"Art. Love. Geology." 154
"August" 42
"Autumn Song" 17

Balbo, Ned 74
"The Ballad of Sadie LaBabe" 85
"Baltimore" 165
Barnstone, Aliki 76
Bashō, Matsua 58
Battiste, Michele 123
Beatty, Jan 67
Becker, Kimberly L. 41
Blaskey, Linda 127
Bosselaar, Laure-Anne 166
Brickman, Sara 195

"A Career Guide for Girls" 139
Cather, Willa 167
Chang, Tina 58
Charara, Hayan 102
Chin Tanner, Wendy 58
"City of Tonawonda Softball Championship" 77
"Commercial Break, Road Runner, Uneasy" 119
"Conviction" 99
Cooper, Wyn 41
Curbelo, Silvia 103

Da', Laura 104
Dawson, Erica 145
de Andrade, Eugenio 167
de la Paz, Oliver 59
Derricotte, Toi 179
"Detroit" 168
"Doña Josefina Counsels Doña Concepción Before Entering Sears" 127
"Dorothy Arzner Looks..." 150
Dunbar, Paul Laurence 60

Eady, Cornelius 168
"Elegy for Brian Wilson's Smile" 182
"Elegy for Iain Banks" 180
"Elegy for my Husband" 179
"Elegy for the Mississippi" 187
"Eletelephony" 19
"Elizabeth and Elaine" 74
"Everyone Has a Story" 81

Fagan, Kathy 42
Fasano, Joseph 90
"Father's Day" 187
"Feast" 69
Ferrell, Monique 197
"Fin" 41
"Fisher Street" 95
"The Fisherman's Wife" 129
"Fly" 170
"Fog" 173
"for bukowski upon hearing of his death" 184

"Fragment 168 B" 44
"Fragments from Childhood" 144
Freligh, Sarah 77
"From Love, Imagination" 45
Frost, Robert 51

Gaines-Friedler, Joy 60, 168
Garren, Christine 39
"Going Deep for Jesus" 67
Gotera, Vince 180
Gottleib, Daphne 192
"Green Ash, Red Maple, Black Gum" 46
Guevara, Maurice Kilwein 127
Guida, George 182

Hall, Hazel 169
"Hat" 35
Henson, Lance 184
"Heraclitean" 90
Hinrichsen, Dennis 184
Hogue, Cynthia 147
Holub, Miroslav 148
Hopkins, Gerard Manley 11
Hopper, Ailish 149
"Hour of Dawn" 59
Hunkley, Tom C. 128

"I wandered lonely as a cloud" 47
"I Want Everything" 113
"In Search of Aunt Jemima" 211
"Innocence" 83
"Interior Divided" 149
Issa 170

"The Jeffrey McDaniel Show" 201
Johnson, Kate Knapp 106
Joseph, Allison 42
"Joyride in Blue" 103
"July 12, 1952: Waiting" 123

"King" 186
Kwon Dobbs, Jennifer 79

"Las Vegas" 61
Lawler, Patick 150
Lawrence, Kathleen A. 186
Lau, Evelyn 61
Lemmon, Amy 187
Leonin, Mia 129
"A Letter from Iceland" 147
"Letter from the Waters of Guantanamo Bay" 195
Leyva, Steven 165
"Like Stars" 19
"Lion and Gin" 184
"Lipstick" 45
Low, Denise 178
Lowell, Amy 44, 164

MacLennan, Amy 130
Masters, Edgar Lee 131
Maybe, Ellyn 199
McDaniel, Jeffrey 201
McDougal, Jo 55
McGee, Lynn 172
McGookey, Kathi 19
"Medusa Cuts her Hair" 132
Meitner, Erika 109
"Mending" 169
Monahan, Jean 132
Moss, Thylias 95

Mossotti, Travis 187
"Mrs. Kessler" 131
Murphy, Erin 81
"My Father Talks of 1946" 133

"The Need to be Versed in
Country Things" 51
"Night" 166
"The Noon Hour" 63
"Notes on Longing" 58

"O Captain! My Captain!" 188
"On Summer" 170
"The Other Woman" 41
"Otis Clay Talks about His
Parents" 127

"Painted Fire" 79
Perdomo, Willie 202
Phillips, Carl 142
"Picasso" 199
"Pied Beauty" 11
"please let me be more than
this" 209
Po, Li 17
"Poem for the Mothers" 204
Pool, Sandy 152
"Potpourri" 62
"Prairie Song" 167
Professor Arturo 204

"Queen Anne's Lace" 50
"The Quiltmaker" 178

Rabearivelo, Jean-Joseph 62
Ramke, Bin 154
"The Red Wheelbarrow" 229
Rhein, Christine 133
"Richard Cory" 82
Richards, Laura Elizabeth 19
Ridge, Lola 62
Robinson, Edward Arlington 82
Roripaugh, Lee Ann 83
"The Ruins" 39

Samyn, Mary Ann 139
Sandburg, Carl 63, 173
Sappho 44
Sarai, Sarah 45
Satterfield, Jane 45
"The Sea at Our Door" 57
Seibles, Tim 85, 119
"Semantics" 145
Seuss, Diane 125
Shankar, Ravi 111
"Should Old Shit be
Forgot" 202
"Since You Ask" 142
"Song for the Sugarcane" 173
"Song of Myself" (1) 17
"Spacetime" 148
"A Study in Bird Song" 152
"Stupid Chicken Falls in
Love" 106
Suarez, Virgil 173
"Summer in the South" 60
"Sunshine" 164

Terman, Phillip 174
"Thinking American" 102
"Too Much Yes" 60
"Translated from the
Night" (7) 62

"Vantage" 104
"Venus Transiens" 44

"Wallflowers" 168
"watch your tense and case" 192
Waters, Michael 46
"Waylon Smithers, Jr." 128
Weigl, Bruce 71
Wesley, Patricia Jabbeh 112
"What Marge Would Say If She Lived" 125
"What Saves Us" 71
"What We Need" 55
"When Nancy Drew the Line" 130
Whitman, Walt 17, 188
Williams, Cee 209
Williams, Crystal 211
Williams, M.L. 35
Williams, William Carlos 49, 50, 229
"Windows" 167
"Winter and War on Lake Monona" 76
"Woman Waiting" 42
Wordsworth, William 47

"The Young Housewife" 49
Yüce, Ali 69

Permissions

"Butter" from *Crave Radiance: New and Selected Poems 1990-2010.* Copyright © 1997 by Elizabeth Alexander. Reprinted with the permission of The Permissions Company, Inc., on behalf of Graywolf Press, www.graywolfpress.org

"The Sea at Our Door" Copyright © 2006 by Joel Allegretti. Reprinted by permission of Joel Allegretti.

"Fragments from Childhood" from *Trouble Sleeping* by Abdul Ali, published by New Issues Poetry & Prose. Copyright © 2015 by Abdul Ali. Reprinted by permission of New Issues Poetry & Prose.

"Conviction" from *Human Nature* copyright © Alice Anderson. Reprinted by permission.

"Elizabeth and Elaine" from *Galileo's Banquet*, published by Washington Writer's Publishing House. Copyright © 1998 by Ned Balbo. Reprinted with permission of Ned Balbo.

"Winter and War on Lake Monona" copyright © Aliki Barnstone. Reprinted by permission of Sheep Meadow Press.

"Untitled" by Matsua Bashō translated by Peter Beilenson. Public Domain.

"July 12, 1952: Waiting" copyright © Michele Battiste. Reprinted by permission of Michele Battiste and Black Lawrence Press.

"Going Deep for Jesus" from *Boneshaker*, by Jan Beatty, © 2002. Reprinted by permission of the University of Pittsburgh Press.

"The Other Woman" from *The Dividings* by Kimberly L. Becker © 2014 Wordtech Communications LLC, Cincinnati, Ohio.

"Otis Clay Talks about his Parents" copyright © 2016 by Linda Blaskey. Reprinted by permission.

"Night" from *Small Gods of Grief.* Copyright © 2001 by Laure Anne Bosselaar. Reprinted with the permission of The Permissions Company, Inc., on behalf of BOA Editions, Ltd., www.boaeditions.org.

"Letter from the Water at Guantanamo Bay" copyright © by Sara Brickman. Reprinted by permission of Sara Brickman. The poem appears in Split This Rock's *The Quarry: A Social Justice Poetry Database.*

"Prairie Song" by Willa Cather. Public domain.

"Notes on Longing" from *Half Lit Houses.* Copyright © 2004 by Tina Chang. Reprinted with the permission of The Permissions Company, Inc., on behalf of Four Way Books, www.fourwaybooks.com

"Thinking American" reprinted from *The Alchemist's Diary* © 2001 by Hayan Charara, by permission of Hanging Loose Press.

"Allzheimer's" from *Turn* copyright © by Wendy Chin Tanner. Reprinted by permission of Wendy Chin Tanner.

"Fin" from *Chaos in the New Calm.* Copyright © 2010 by Wyn Cooper. Reprinted with the permission of The Permissions Company, Inc., on behalf of BOA Editions, Ltd., www.boaeditions.com

"Joyride in Blue" from *Falling Landscapes* by Silvia Curbelo. Copyright © 2015 Anghinga Press. Reprinted with permission of Anghinga Press and Silvia Curbelo.

"Vantage" from *Tributaries* written by Laura Da' and published by the University of Arizona Press. Copyright © 2015 Laura Da'. Reprinted by permission of Laura Da'.

"Semantics" from *Big Eyed Afraid.* Reprinted by kind permission of the author and The Waywiser Press (http://waywiser press.com)

"Windows" written by Eugenio de Andrade and translated by Alexis Levitin. Published in *Close to Speech* by Red Dancefloor Press. Copyright © Alexis Levitin. Reprinted by permission of Alexis Levitin.

"Hour of Dawn" appears in *Furious Lullaby* by Oliver de la Paz. Copyright © 2007 by Oliver de la Paz. Reprinted by permission of Southern Illinios University Press and Oliver de la Paz.

"Elegy for my Husband" Copyright © 2012 by Toi Derricotte. Reprinted by permission.

"Painted Fire" from *Paper Pavilion.* Copyright © 2007 by Jennifer Kwon Dobbs. Reprinted with permission of White Pine Press and Jennifer Kwon Dobbs.

"Summer in the South" by Paul Laurence Dunbar. Public Domain.

"Wallflowers" by Cornelius Eady from *Victims of the Latest Dance Craze.* Used with permission of Cornelius Eady.

"August" from *The Charm* by Kathy Fagan. Copyright © 2002 by Kathy Fagan. Reprinted with permission.

"Heraclitean" from *Inheritance* by Joseph Fasano. Copyright © 2014 by Cider Press Review. Reprinted with permission.

"airtight alibi" copyright © Monique Ferrell. Reprinted by permission of Monique Ferell.

"City of Tonawanda Softball Championship" Copyright © 2008 by Sarah Freligh. First published by Turning Point Books in *Sort of Gone.* Reprinted with permission of Sarah Freligh.

"The Need to be Versed in Country Things" by Robert Frost. Public Domain.

"Detroit" copyright © Joy Gaines Friedler. Reprinted by permission.

"Too Much Yes" from *Like Vapor* by Joy Gaines Friedler. Copyright © Joy Gaines Friedler. Reprinted by permission of Joy Gaines Friedler and Mayapple Press.

"The Ruins" from *Among the Monarchs* by Christine Garren. Reprinted by permission of the University of Chicago Press. © 2000 by The University of Chicago. All rights reserved.

"Elegy for Iain Banks" by Vince Gotera. Copyright © Vince Gotera. Reprinted by permission.

"watch your tense and case" from *Pelt* by Daphne Gottlieb, published in 1999 by Odd Girls Press. Copyright © Daphne Gottlieb and reprinted with permission of author.

"Doña Josefina Counsels Doña Concepción Before Entering Sears" from *Poems of the River Spirit*, by Maurice Kilwein Guevara, © 1996. Reprinted by permission of the University of Pittsburgh Press.

"Elegy for Brian Wilson's Happiness." Copyright © 2016 by George Guida. Reprinted by permission.

"Mending" by Hazel Hall. Public domain.

"for bukoski upon hearing of his death" from *Strong Heart Song: Lines from a Revolutionary Text* by Lance Henson. Copyright © West End Press. Reprinted with permission.

"Lion and Gin" from *Kurosawa's Dog* by Dennis Hinrichsen. Copyright © 2009 by Dennis Hinrichsen. Reprinted by permission of Oberlin College Press and Dennis Hinrichsen.

"Letter from Iceland" from *The Never Wife* published by MAMMOTH books. Copyright © 1999 by Cynthia Hogue. Reprinted by permission of Cynthia Hogue.

"Spacetime" from *Intensive Care: New and Selected Poems* written by Miroslav Holub and translated by David Young. Copyright © 1996 by Oberlin College Press. Reprinted by permission.

"Pied Beauty" by Gerard Manley Hopkins. Public Domain.

"Divided Interior" from *Dark~Sky Society* by Ailish Hopper, published by New Issues Poetry & Prose. Copyright © 2014 by Ailish Hopper. Reprinted by permission of New Issues Poetry & Prose.

"On Summer" by George Moses Horton. Public Domain.

"Waylon Smithers, Jr." copyright © 2015 by Tom C. Hunley. Reprinted by permission of Split Lip Press.

Untitled by Issa. Translated by Peter Beilenson. Public domain.

"Stupid Chicken Falls in Love with Pick Up Truck" from *This Perfect Life* by Kate Knapp Johnson. Copyright © 1993 by Miami University Press. Reprinted by permission.

"Woman Waiting" Copyright © by Allison Joseph. Reprinted by permission.

"Rookeries and Red Wheelbarrows" from *Palpable Magic* by Gerry LaFemina. Copyright © 2015 by Stephen F. Austin University Press. Reprinted by permission.

"Dorothy Arzner Looks in the Lens of her Camera and Sees Caroline Herschel's Comets Falling through Adrienne Rich's Eyes" Copyright © 2006 Patrik Lawler. Reprinted by permission of Patrick Lawler and Many Mountain Moving Press.

"Las Vegas" from *Grain of Rice*, published by Oolichan Books. Copyright © 2012 by Evelyn Lau.

"King" copyright © 2016 by Kathleen Lawrence. Reprinted with permission.

"Father's Day" copyright © 2016 by Amy Lemmon. Reprinted by permission.

"The Fisherman's Wife" from *Unraveling the Bed* © Mia Leonin. Reprinted with permission of Anhinga Press.

"Baltimore" by Steven Leyva from *Low Parish* (Toad Sage Press, 2012). Used with permission of the author and publisher.

"The Quiltmaker" from *New and Selected Poems* (Penthe Publishing, 1999). Copyright © 1999 by Denise Low. Reprinted by permission of Denise Low.

"Sunshine" and "Venus Transiens" by Amy Lowell. Public Domain.

"When Nancy Drew the Line" copyright © by Amy MacLennan. Reprinted by permission of Amy MacLennan.

"Mrs. Kessler" by Edgar Lee Masters. Public Domain.

"Picasso" by Ellyn Maybe. Used with permission of the author.

"The Jeffrey McDaniel Show" © 2002 by Jeffrey McDaniel, from *The Splinter Factory* (Manic D Press: San Francisco). Reprinted by permission of author and publisher.

"What We Need" from *Home of the Famous Dead* by Jo McDougall. Copyright © 2015 by Jo McDougall. Reprinted by permission of the University of Arkansas Press.

"Fly" copyright © by Lynn McGee. Reprinted by permission of Lynn McGee and Bright Hill Press, Inc. (First published in *Heirloom Bulldog*, Bright Hill Press).

"Like Stars" from *Stay* (Press 53) Copyright © 2015 by Kathi McGookey. Used with permission.

"Apartment" from *Inventory at the All Night Drugstore* © Erika Meitner. Reprinted with permission of Anhinga Press.

"Medusa Cuts her Hair" from *Believe It or Not* by Jean Monahan, published by Orchises Press, and reprinted by permission.

"Fisher Street" by Thylias Moss from *Pyramid of Bone* copyright © 1989 Thylias Moss. Used with permission of the University of Virginia Press.

"Elegy for the Mississippi" copyright © by Travis Mossotti. Reprinted by permission of Travis Mossotti.

"Everyone has a Story" appeared originally in *Pennsylvania English* and appears in *Science of Desire* by Erin Murphy, Word Press, Cincinnati, OH 2004. Copyright © by Erin Murphy.

"Poem for the Mothers" from *My Name is New Orleans: 40 Years of Poetry & Other Jazz.* Copyright © 2009 Arthur Pfister aka Professor Arturo. Reprinted with permission of Arthur Pfister and Margaret Media, Inc.

"Should Old Shit be Forgot" originally published in *Smoking Lovely* by Willie Perdomo, published by Rattapallax Press. Copyright © 2005 by Willie Perdomo. Used by permission of Willie Perdomo.

"Since You Ask" copyright © by Carl Phillips. Reprinted by permission.

"Autumn River Song" by Li Po as translated by Sam Hamill. Copyright © Sam Hamill. Reprinted by permission of Sam Hamill.

"A Study of Bird Song" copyright © by Sandy Pool. Reprinted by permission.

"Translated from the Night #7" from *Translated From the Night*, written by Jean-Joseph Rabearivelo and translated by Robert Ziller. Copyright © 2007 by Lascaux Editions. Reprinted by permission.

"Art. Love. Geology." *from Massacre of the Innocents: Poems* by Bin Ramke. Copyright © 1995 by Bin Ramke. Reprinted by permission of Bin Ramke and Univeristy of Iowa Press.

"My Father Talks of 1946" Copyright © by Christine Rhein from *Wild Flight*, Texas Tech University Press. Reprinted by permission.

"Eletelephony" by Laura Elizabeth Richards. Public domain.

"Potpourri" by Lola Ridge. Public Domain.

"Richard Cory" by Edward Arlington Robinson. Public domain.

"Innocence" appears in *Year of the Snake* by Lee Ann Roripaugh. Copyright © 2004 by Lee Ann Roripaugh. Reprinted by permission of Southern Illinois University Press.

"A Career Guide for Girls" from *Inside the Yellow Dress* by Mary Ann Samyn, published by New Issues Poetry & Press. Copyright © 2001 by Mary Ann Samyn. Reprinted by permission of New Issues Poetry & Press.

"Fog" and "The Noon Hour" by Carl Sandburg. Public Domain.

"168 B from Sappho's Lyre" translated by Diane Raynor from *Sappho's Lyre: Archaic Lyric and Women Poets of Ancient Greece.* © 1991 by Diane Rayor. Published by the University of California Press, 65.

"From Love, Imagination" by Sarah Sarai. Copyright © by Sarah Sarai. Published in *Boston Review*, 35:4; 2011. Reprinted by permission.

"Lipstick" from *Shepherdess with Automatic* copyright © Jane Satterfield. Reprinted by permission of Washington Writers Publishing House.

"The Ballad of Sadie Lababe" Copyright © by Tim Seibles. Reprinted by permission of Cleveland State University Poetry Center.

"Road Runner, Commercial Break, Uneasy" Copyright © by Tim Seibles. Reprinted by permission of Cleveland State University Poetry Center.
"What Marge would Say if She Lived" copyright © by Diane Seuss. Reprinted by permission of Diane Seuss. First printed in *Poemeleon*.
"Along the River of Palms" copyright © Ravi Shankar. Reprinted by permission of Carolina Wren Press and Ravi Shankar.
"Song to the Sugar Cane" from *Palm Crows* by Virgil Suarez. © 2001 Virgil Suarez. Reprinted by permission of the University of Arizona Press.
"The Architect" from *Rabbis of the Air*. Copyright © 2007 by Philip Terman. Reprinted by permission of Autumn House Press.
"Green Ash, Red Maple, Black Gum" from *Parhenopi: New & Selected Poems*. Copyright © 2001 by Michael Waters. Reprinted by permission of The Permission Company, Inc., on behalf of BOA Editions, Ltd., www.boaeditions.com
"What Saves Us" from *What Saves Us* by Bruce Weigl. Copyright © 1992 by Bruce Weigl. Reprinted by permission of Bruce Weigl and Triquarterly Books; Northwestern University Press.
"I Want Everything" copyright © Patricia Jabbeh Wesley. Reprinted by permission of Patricia Jabbeh Wesley.
"O Captain! My Captain" and "Song of Myself" by Walt Whitman. Public Domain.
"Please let me be more than this" copyright © 2015 by Cee Williams. Reprinted by permission.
"In Search of Aunt Jemima" copyright © by Crystal A. Williams. Reprinted by permission of Crystal A. Williams.
"Hat" Copyright © 2016 by M. L. Williams. Reprinted by permission by M. L. Williams.
"Queen Anne's Lace," "The Red Wheel Barrow," and "The Young Housewife" by William Carlos Williams. Public Domain.
"Feast" from *Voice Lock Puppet* by Ali Yüce, published by Orchises Press and reprinted by permission.

CPSIA information can be obtained
at www.ICGtesting.com
Printed in the USA
FSHW021644041220
76587FS